2803

The
Formative
Years

The Formative Years

Gordon Trasler

John Bowlby

Penelope Leach

Colin Hindley

Basil Bernstein

David M. Downes

British Broadcasting Corporation

Published by the
British Broadcasting Corporation
35 Marylebone High Street
London W.1

SBN: 563 07404 3

First published 1968

© Gordon Trasler, John Bowlby,
Penelope Leach, Colin Hindley,
Basil Bernstein and
David M. Downes 1968

Printed in England by
Cox & Wyman Ltd, London,
Reading and Fakenham

Contents

NOTES ON CONTRIBUTORS

GORDON TRASLER is Professor of Psychology in the University of Southampton. His principal publications include *In Place of Parents – a Short Study of Foster Care* (1960) and *The Explanation of Criminality* (1962).

JOHN BOWLBY is Director of the Department for Children and Parents, and of the Child Development Research Unit at the Tavistock Clinic in London. He is the author of *Personal Aggressiveness and War* (1944) and *Maternal Care and Mental Health* (1950), which he wrote for the World Health Organization.

PENELOPE LEACH is Assistant Lecturer in Social Psychology at the London School of Economics. Her publications include 'A study of the literature concerning rigidity' *British Journal of Social and Clinical Psychology* (1967), and many other articles.

COLIN HINDLEY is Director of research and Senior Lecturer at the Centre for the Study of Human Development at London University. He is also co-editor of the *Journal of Child Psychology and Psychiatry*, and the author of many articles.

DAVID DOWNES is a Lecturer in Social Administration at the London School of Economics, and review editor of the *British Journal of Criminology*. He is the author of *The Delinquent Solution* (1966) and of many articles.

BASIL BERNSTEIN is Reader in the Sociology of Education at the University of London Institute of Education.

DAVID EDGE was the BBC producer responsible for the original series. He is now Director of the Science Studies Unit, University of Edinburgh.

Preface

By the age of three years (as Professor Hermann Bondi has remarked) we have all learned as much physics as we will ever learn again: that is to say, we quickly build up a 'working knowledge' of our physical environment, and this pattern, so early established, forms the basis of our later, more sophisticated, understanding.

Can the same kind of claim be made of our grasp of social relationships, and the formation of our personalities? 'The Formative Years', originally broadcast in the BBC Third Programme, presented some recent thinking on the forces which mould our development, and the processes by which they take effect.

The series was not intended to cover all aspects of current research; some significant theorizing (such as Dr R. D. Laing's analysis of the family context) had, for various reasons, to be omitted. What was eventually broadcast, and is here published, took the form of a collection of samples. Professor Trasler's introductory summary makes further preface unnecessary: if what follows brings some insight into the reader's familiar context, and gives him, through inner understanding, greater access to himself, then the purposes of those who compiled these samples will have been well served.

DAVID EDGE
Director, Science Studies Unit,
Edinburgh University

Gordon Trasler

Socialization

It is apparent that what is called 'the socialization process' is a very complex thing indeed. If one were to attempt to make a list of all the skills, habits, and items of information which an individual must learn if he is to become a competent member of our society, the result would be impossibly unwieldy and certainly incomplete. Fortunately such an exercise is by no means essential to an understanding of the nature of the process. It is simpler, and much more illuminating, to consider the types or styles of learning which contribute to the socialization of the child.

We can usefully begin by making a distinction between two essentially different processes. One of these consists in the acquisition of techniques: the basic human technique of language, the recognition and categorization of physical objects, the use of an immense variety of tools, and the social skills involved in perceiving the attitudes of others and in making appropriate verbal and behavioural responses to them. This sort of learning equips the child with what may be called 'problem-solutions' – it teaches him how to carry out his intentions, how to reach the objectives which are desirable to him. It appears to follow the familiar principle of reward; correct actions, which lead to the desired result, are remembered and repeated, while unsuccessful ways of doing things are discarded. But the other sort of learning is different in purpose; it is the means by which the child develops those emotional reactions of admiration, aversion, guiltiness, and so on which will underlie and motivate his social behaviour. A young child, as every parent knows, is not naturally quiet or clean or respectful. He has to be trained to inhibit several kinds of behaviour which, to begin with, are part of his natural repertoire. Nor does he naturally exhibit the reverence for social symbols and badges of status which, to adults, are such strong motives, and the source of so much satisfaction – and, of course, frustration.

Because most investigators of early social learning have been particularly interested in delinquency, a great deal of attention has been paid to the negative reactions of aversion and guilt which serve to inhibit certain types of anti-social behaviour; this part of the socialization process is often referred to as 'anxiety conditioning'. Provided we remember that other more positive emotional reactions are acquired in the course of the same process, this oversimplification is not a serious matter, and indeed it serves to emphasize two important aspects of emotional learning which distinguish it sharply from the acquisition of skills and problem-solutions.

First, it is clearly not a matter of learning by results – of reward and punishment in the conventional sense – but of association; it depends upon the conjunction of a state of aversion or anxiety with a particular action or impulse, just as Pavlovian conditioning relies upon the relationship in time between salivation and some kind of signal. The emotional reactions which control our social behaviour are often loosely described as 'instinctive' – meaning, I think, that they are elicited automatically, usually without prior reflection, and often without any clear awareness of their origin. Certain situations just seem to us to be inherently disgusting, certain actions to be 'unthinkable', and certain goals to be intrinsically desirable, so that it takes a considerable effort to grasp the fact that these are learned reactions and not inherent characteristics of the situation itself. An aversion to violence, for instance, has little to do with the probable outcome of a violent act – with whether or not it will prove to be profitable; rather, it is an emotional state evoked by those elements of a situation (or an anticipated situation) which we have been trained to associate with guilt or disgrace.

The other virtue of the anxiety-conditioning parallel is that it draws attention to the *mediating* rôle of the emotional reaction. It is frequently triggered off by a stimulus which the individual himself produces, by recognizing certain specific aspects of a social situation, or by contemplating a particular course of action which he might take, and it then has the effect of motivating (or more often, of inhibiting) behaviour. It is interesting to note that where mediating emotional reactions of this kind have been induced in laboratory animals, as in the famous experiments by Solomon and Wynne upon conditioned fear in dogs, they have been found to be virtually permanent. Unlike ordinary skills and habits, which must be periodically rehearsed and rewarded if they are not to decay, acquired emotional reactions seem to maintain their effectiveness indefinitely, with little or no reinforcement, once they have been established.

According to this view, then, social training consists in the conditioning of new emotional reactions in such a way that, on future occasions, they will control or modify the child's behaviour. Let us take a simple example – training a child not to steal. What usually seems to happen is that in the normal pursuit of childish interests the child helps himself to a sweet or a toy or some other desirable object, is seen to do so, and is rebuked or mildly punished by his parents. Episodes like this are repeated a few times until eventually the child 'learns' (as we say) 'to respect other people's property' – by which we mean, I think, that he has developed an aversion to those behaviours which have been defined for him as 'stealing'. He now feels extremely uncomfortable if he does take something that he knows is not his, and if you detect him at it you will often find guilt written all over his face.

It is a common mistake to suppose that what the child has learned is to anticipate punishment, but this is not an adequate account of the matter. Most of us have a positive and irrational dislike of certain proscribed behaviours, an aversion which persists even in situations in which there is no possibility of punishment. Such attitudes are not confined to adults, as any teacher will confirm. If, for example, a purse is missing from the cloakroom, it is the usual thing to address the class sternly and to demand that the thief should own up. When this happens several children can be relied upon to blush and to look extremely uncomfortable, even though they could have had nothing to do with the theft. In point of fact they are generally the most moral and highly-socialized of children; more often than not the culprit himself sits with an expression of beaming innocence, quite untouched by the anxiety which disturbs his law-abiding fellows.

This type of emotional response is learned, as we have seen, through the repeated association of a certain class of actions with some device which will reliably elicit anxiety or guilt — that is to say, some sanction. It is worth emphasizing that the sanctions used in child training are not punishments in Thorndike's sense — they are effective, not because they represent the unpleasant outcome of a specific sequence of actions, but because they are capable of arousing an emotional reaction. It is the resurgence of this reaction which blocks the activity on future occasions, not the anticipation of pain.

What has all this to do with child development? The point, I think, is that by far the most effective vehicle for eliciting an emotional reaction in a young child is his dependency upon his parents. There is no need to labour the fact that this relationship is the source of immense satisfaction, and its temporary withdrawal can be relied upon to elicit quite severe anxiety. All parents make use of these facts to mould the child's behaviour; as a rule physical punishments and tangible rewards (if they are used at all) are effective largely as tokens or demonstrations of parental disfavour or disapproval. This suggests two aspects of the child training process which are likely to be of key importance: the quality of the dependent relation between the child and his parents, and the consistency with which they exploit this as a sanction. In the extreme case of total privation of maternal care, no pattern of dependency has ever been established. As, therefore, the mode of child training which I have described is not available, we should expect socialization to be severely retarded in such cases, at least during the first six or seven years of life. If, on the other hand, the dependent relationship is interrupted after it has been established, or is so unreliable and unsatisfactory to the child that temporary clouding of parental approval has no specific meaning for him, some degree of interference with the normal process of socialization is inevitable. As Dr Bowlby was able to show in his classic review of studies of maternal deprivation, these contentions are well supported by empirical evidence.

But although the parent-child relationship is obviously of central importance, it is not the only vehicle of social training. In due course the child joins a neighbourhood play group and school groups, and he develops another mode of dependency, upon peer relations. This supplements, and to some extent gradually supplants, his relationship with his parents; and this peer-dependency is the source of new sanctions, a new sensitiveness to group disapproval, which emphatically plays a part in socialization. But not all children have the same social experience. It appears, for example, that among middle-class families in contemporary British society the period of exclusive dependence upon the parents is comparatively long, and yields only gradually to reliance upon peer-relations; but in working-class neighbourhoods dependence upon the peer-group is established much earlier, and plays a more important part in the first phases of social training. I think it is probable that the characteristic middle-class determination to exercise as much control as possible over the child's activity, in order to mould his character, is at the root of these differences; but they must be, at least to some extent, determined by the sort of neighbourhood in which families live. It is difficult, if not impossible, to restrict casual contacts with people outside the family in a high-density working-class district, although it is easy in a typical suburban neighbourhood, with its defensive system of fences, hedges and garden gates.

There is good reason to believe that the middle-class style of child rearing, deliberately exploiting a prolonged, exclusive parent-child relationship in what is sometimes called 'love-oriented discipline', is the more effective means of emotional conditioning. When virtually all of the child's social experience, and the whole of his emotional dependency, are concentrated within the confines of the family, his training can be carried through with maximum intensity and consistency. This is probably one reason why middle-class families seem to produce a relatively small number of detected delinquents – though it is not the whole explanation, as we shall see.

There is another interesting consequence of these differences in the patterns of child rearing. Children who are accustomed to gain virtually all of their comfort and reassurance from a very few intense and dependable two-person relationships are likely to look for similar relationships at each stage of their development. On the other hand, a child who learns quite early in life to depend upon his age-peers for the satisfaction of his basic social needs (and this is the normal pattern in some working-class groups) is likely to grow up much more sensitive to group pressures and group disapproval. He may indeed be relatively indifferent to the sort of two-person, dependent relationships which are so significant to his middle-class counterpart. This fact is of the first importance in planning the re-training of delinquents, and it is often overlooked. We continue to put some offenders whose social satisfactions have been almost entirely derived from the peer-group into the care of individual probation officers and borstal house-masters, while we plunge middle-class delinquents, with quite different backgrounds of social experience, into group-oriented institutions, with far too little thought for their personal styles of dependency.

One question which has been much discussed in recent years is whether or not substantial deprivation of parental care during infancy and early childhood is likely to result in permanent damage to personality development – and, if so, in what conditions. Early attempts to answer these questions did not give sufficient attention to the nature and sequence of social experiences in general, or of dependency-relations in particular. But the extent to which an individual will succeed in attaining full membership of his peer group, in school or in neighbourhood play, appears to be to a large degree determined by the quality of his earlier relationships within the family – by whether he has learned there the interpersonal skills and confidence in relationships with others that are necessary to him as a member of a group. Because of the subcultural differences to which I have referred, the timing of this sequence of social experiences is substantially different in one social group from that to be found in another – a fact which must surely be taken into account in any study of the effects of deprivation. The nature of the handicap which will result from deprivation will clearly depend upon the phase of his social development, so defined, which the child has reached at the time of the separation. Perhaps even more important, the extent to which the handicap will be immediately evident, and the possibility of the child 'catching up' on his social development, are likely to depend to a considerable degree upon the kind of substitute relationship which he is offered – whether, for example, it is with parent-substitutes of the orthodox kind or within a small social group in which peer relations predominate. These questions are of interest to the student of delinquency because of the close connexions which appear to exist between the child's responsiveness to social training and his capacity (and desire) for dependent relationships of various kinds. This is a matter to which we shall return in due course.

But first let us look briefly at another implication of the anxiety-conditioning model which served as a framework for our earlier discussion. The acquired emotional reactions upon which socialization is based will not, of course, function effectively unless the child is able to identify those situations which should trigger off the response; the cognitive aspect of social conditioning is thus of key importance. Training a child to have an aversion to stealing, for example, is pointless if you do not also teach him to distinguish accurately between this category of behaviour and other kinds of actions which are not regarded as stealing. How is this discrimination problem dealt with? Parents who are trying to train their children often make use of verbal explanations to structure the situation; these may be simple, or they may be highly sophisticated. A father who wants to restrain his noisy son may give him a sharp smack and say 'Shut up!' – a remark which gives no more than a general indication that he is being a nuisance. The child is left to divine, if he can, what it is that he is doing wrong. Another parent, in a similar situation, will say something of this kind: 'I wouldn't shout like that if I were you; you're upsetting mummy, and you don't want to give her a headache, do you? In any case, we can hear you much better if you speak quietly.' It is obvious, I think, that these different approaches to the task of teaching the child to discriminate will not have the same result.

Dr Basil Bernstein, who is contributing to this series, has devised an ingenious analysis of types of language which is particularly relevant to this matter. His argument is a complex and rather technical one, and I shall not attempt to anticipate it here. But its implications for the point now at issue can be stated in a few words. Bernstein bases his analysis upon the distinction between 'restricted codes' of language, consisting of short, simple sentences, often in the form of categoric statements, and essentially concrete in character – and 'elaborated' language, which is more precise, is relatively complex in syntactical structure, employs abstract terms, and tends to be cast in syllogistic form (that is to say, identifying premises and consequences). He argues, and cites evidence to show, that there are marked differences between the social classes and between people of different educational backgrounds in respect of the use which they make of these two forms of language. People in working-class neighbourhoods use the simple, direct, concrete 'restricted codes' almost exclusively; middle-class people of good education use both types of language, but prefer the elaborated form when they have something important to say.

It is clear, I think, that parents who are accustomed to using elaborated speech will find it easier to explain to their children which are the significant characteristics of an action and which are irrelevant – they are more precise and more articulate. But it is not merely a matter of verbal facility; the use of elaborated codes implies the habit of thinking in terms of principles, generalizations and reasons, and it is likely that these intellectual skills are developed through the use of language. A parent who explains carefully to her child what it is that he has done wrong does not simply convey a particular prohibition; she also trains him to look for general principles and reasons, and to perceive his own behaviour and his own intentions in these terms.

This is of some significance to our discrimination problem. As Pavlov demonstrated in his laboratory, the basic requirement for conditioning is that an identifiable signal should be repeatedly followed by the response that you want the subject to learn. The signal has to be made to stand out from the background 'noise' of the situation. A good way of bringing this about is to present the same signal in several different contexts. This variation of background happens naturally in social training, if parents manage things in the right way. Any normal child breaks a number of social taboos in the course of a single day. He may chase the cat, thump the child next

B

door, pull the dog's tail, and tease his baby sister – this would be a comparatively light day's programme for an average five-year-old. If each misdemeanour is visited by a simple rebuke, without explanation, he will accumulate four rather vague notions about things he must not do. If, on the other hand, each of these actions is defined for him as 'being cruel', he has four opportunities for learning the same lesson. One would expect him to have developed some skill in distinguishing cruel behaviour from other sorts of action, and he should have acquired at least a rudimentary aversion to any activity which fits this description. General principles are readily transferred from one event or occasion to another, and so facilitate the establishment of powerful and reliable emotional responses; they also furnish a frame of reference that has meaning in novel situations, so that the child is able to respond appropriately to circumstances which he has not previously encountered.

Bernstein's work on group differences in the use of language has some connexions with another line of research, concerned with variations in parents' attitudes to bringing up their children. Sociological studies have shown that middle-class parents (and some working-class parents) tend to regard bringing up a family as a difficult, rather hazardous procedure which demands much attention and forethought if it is to be successfully accomplished. On the other hand, many parents in the lower working class (that is to say, unskilled workers and their wives) take a far more relaxed, casual view of their rôle; they tend to the belief that, given a certain minimum of care and control, children will naturally grow up to be ordinary healthy adults. These alternative views of parenthood lead to different reactions when the child misbehaves. In one family a five-year-old who abstracts a jam tart when his mother is not looking may be given a mild smack or an indulgent dig in the ribs, because this sort of behaviour is considered natural in a child of his age – but in another family the same action will be treated with great seriousness. It may be only a jam tart, it is argued, but the child must be made to learn the distinction between what is his and what is not, or he will grow up to be a thief.

There is some evidence that these differences in parental attitudes are beginning to disappear. The rather grim emphasis upon character training that was typical of middle-class families of a generation or so ago is now much less in evidence, while on the other hand concern for the child's long-term development has become characteristic of most working-class parents. There are probably several reasons for this, one of which is certainly the increased influence of books and magazine articles dealing with methods and problems of bringing up children. The marked inequalities of education, income and style of life which used to differentiate occupational and social classes have greatly diminished, and this is bound to have a profound effect upon patterns of socialization. Social changes of this kind are of particular interest to criminologists, for the relatively high incidence of detected crime among people from lower working-class homes has often been explained, plausibly enough, in terms of the kinds of differences we have been considering – differences in attitudes to parenthood, in the use of language to communicate precepts and values, and in willingness to make use of 'love-oriented' methods of discipline. If these differences become eroded we may expect the class differentials in crime rates to disappear too. It will be interesting to see whether this happens.

But, as I remarked earlier, it is unlikely that the relation between social class and aberrant social behaviour can be wholly accounted for by differences in styles of child upbringing. Oddly enough, one of the most recalcitrant pieces of evidence comes from studies in individual differences. It is admittedly a difficult matter to obtain reliable information about the abilities and attainments of delinquents and the educational opportunities which they have enjoyed. But we now have fairly satisfactory evidence that young offenders tend to be 'under-achievers' – by which is meant that their educational attainments are poorer than their measured intellectual status would lead one to expect. The argument we have been pursuing suggests a two-fold explanation for this fact. We know that a large proportion of those who are convicted of such 'orthodox' crimes as thefts and breaking offences are drawn from lower working-class families – that is to say, from families in which 'elaborated codes' of speech are seldom employed. Following Bernstein's reasoning, we should expect such individuals to be at a considerable disadvantage in an educational system in which such language is the normal mode of interaction between teacher and pupil. Thus the existence of a general correlation between under-achievement and delinquency can be partly accounted for in terms of the social-class origins of offenders.

But this does not dispose of the problem, for we know that only a minority of boys from lower working-class families are brought before the courts as delinquents. These, interestingly enough, show as a group a much greater disparity between ability and attainment than do non-delinquent boys from the same stratum. Why should this be so? The answer to this question is to be found, I think, in the connexion between language development and socialization which we have examined. Because the effectiveness of emotional conditioning partly depends upon the skill with which parents use verbal cues to structure the training situation for their children, we should expect that within any defined social group those families in which verbal intercourse was least precise and sophisticated would fail most frequently as agents of socialization. This seems indeed to be the case, giving support to the contention that both social training (in the narrow sense) and the capacity to respond to formal education depend upon the acquisition of certain basic language skills; if these are lacking the child is likely to become delinquent and also to fail in school.

Nor is this discrepancy between ability and formal educational attainment characteristic only of young delinquents; it has been repeatedly demonstrated in groups of recidivist adult offenders. It is interesting to note, too, that evidence of a marked association between linguistic inadequacy and delinquency has been found in another area of psychological research – the series of investigations of children brought up in old-fashioned residential institutions which were carried out in the United States of America by Goldfarb, Lowrey and others. Here the connexion seems, at first sight, to be of an entirely different kind. It is sometimes suggested that children left to converse among themselves, without adults, employ very crude language which exhibits little development. This seems a reasonable proposition to apply to communities in which there is no interaction with adults at all, but such an extreme condition did not obtain in Goldfarb's institutions; there appears, on the contrary, to have been a fair amount of speech between children and adults, as well as among the children. But what was characteristic of these children's homes was the lack of warm, exclusive, dependent relationships between *particular* children and particular adults, and this seems to have been a crucial defect in the régime as a developmental environment. This work underlines, I think, the key rôle, in the early stages of speech development, of the stimulation and encouragement which derives from satisfying parent-child relationships; some of the other studies to which I have referred give more than a hint that the connexion between language development and emotional conditioning continues to be extremely important throughout childhood. The relationship is a reciprocal one; the nature of the bond between the child and his parents (or parent-substitutes), and with his age-peers, has much to do with determining the rate and direction in which his linguistic powers develop. On the other hand, the precision of his grasp of language considerably colours his social experiences and his interpersonal relations.

That there is a link between anti-social behaviour and lack of competence in social relationships (especially in close affectional relations) is a familiar and well-documented fact. But there has been a certain amount of confusion about the way in which this association should be accounted for. Theorists of the 'dynamic' schools have naturally tended to regard it as one of cause and effect, arguing that delinquency is a reaction to frustrations in personal relationships – a substitute activity. They have pointed out that much delinquent behaviour can be convincingly described as symbolic of such needs and frustrations. But although this view is in accordance with the general emphasis of dynamic psychology upon the primacy of interpersonal relations, it is not the only possible explanation, and not the most parsimonious. The argument from learning theory which we have reviewed implies a different causal connexion, with two strands. First, it asserts that those social experiences, within and without the family, which constitute opportunities to learn the skills of interpersonal relations (and to acquire confidence in them) are also the vehicles of social and 'moral' training, so that the individual whose early experiences within the family are unsatisfactory is doubly handicapped. He will not acquire normal social motives and anxieties; he is also deprived of opportunities for learning the technical skills of social intercourse. Second, this theoretical scheme implies that an individual whose learning in respect of interpersonal skills has been grossly defective will continue to be comparatively invulnerable to social pressures of one kind and another, and is likely therefore to remain under-socialized.

This connexion between delinquency and incompetence in interpersonal relationships has, of course, a number of important implications for the treatment and re-training of offend s. But it has other consequences for the development of the individual child, perhaps long before he is officially identified as a delinquent. Part of the problem is illustrated by the activities and effects of those transient adolescent groups which are usually (though perhaps inaccurately, as Dr Downes will contend in his contribution to this series) referred to as 'gangs'. Albert Cohen suggests that groups of this type are usually composed of individuals who are already conscious of failure in a highly competitive society. In his account of the American scene, the 'bottom of the heap' (as he calls it) is defined largely in terms of underprivileged social origins and lack of acquaintance with middle-class norms and values in a society in which these are important obstacles to upward social mobility. In our society, with its rather more equal opportunities for educational advancement, failure is probably more closely related to sheer educational backwardness. Even in Britain it is a gross oversimplification to identify lack of progress at the primary stage of education with poor intelligence. But there is undoubtedly a strong association between incompetence in the use of language and educational failure. So, following Cohen's argument, we may expect adolescent 'gangs' to be composed of individuals who are to some degree selected by their linguistic inadequacies, and thus (according to our earlier argument) characterized by relative incompetence in interpersonal relations. These facts seem likely, on the face of it, to have a considerable influence upon the nature of social interaction in peer-groups, and indeed Bernstein has produced some evidence to show that verbal intercourse within a group of this kind is almost exclusively confined to the 'restricted' form of speech, with its relative crudity of expression and lack of logical structure.

This may sound a rather trivial point, but I suspect that it is not. For at least some of those individuals who form the 'gang', it is an important agent of socialization. They are – for the reasons I have outlined – people whose characteristic mode of dependency is upon the peer-group, with little investment in two-person, parent-child relations, and they tend to be individuals whose socialization has been retarded. Cohen has argued that in these circumstances membership of an adolescent peer-group is of great significance to the personal security of those who comprise it; respect for its values – a marked tendency to internalize its standards – is common to all of them. In view of Bernstein's work, we should not be surprised at Cohen's discovery that the *mores* of such adolescent groups constitute a simple, black-and-white, unreasoned value-system, implying emphatic rejection of certain prescriptive standards of the middle-class-dominated external society and an unquestioning loyalty to the group. These are, of course, some of the characteristics which make the spontaneous peer-group so much more efficient as an agent of socialization than other adolescent social groups, such as those organized by adults.

These facts have rather sombre implications. Perhaps the most serious is that the individual who becomes dependent upon a peer group of this kind continues to participate in a culture which is notably lacking in opportunities for learning the kinds of precise discrimination, the grasp of abstract principles, and the modes of logical reasoning upon which social competence and sensitive response to other human beings (and to the norms of social conduct) partly depend. For some, indeed, whose early social learning was seriously defective or incomplete, this group experience can be actively disabling, reinforcing patterns of language and thought which are inconsistent with effective functioning in a complex society.

*   *   *

One usually thinks of the socialization process as a mechanism of communication between one generation and the next – as a way of passing on, from parents to children, the framework of rules and precepts which is necessary to the functioning of a stable society. But it is more than this. To-day's children will in due course become the parents of the next generation; they have to acquire for themselves these elements of culture, but they must also learn how to transmit them to their own children. The rudiments of parental be-haviour and parental attitudes are learned in childhood, by direct experience. Even in a highly literate society such as our own, in which young parents are exposed to a considerable volume of printed and broadcast advice about bringing up children, the way in which a mother sees her parental rôle (though not, perhaps, the detailed techniques of management she uses) is still coloured by her recollections of her own childhood.

But we must be careful not to overstate this conservative element in the transmission of culture. Attitudes to parent-hood do change, to a limited extent, from one generation to another, and in the last two or three decades these modifica-tions have been quite marked. We cannot be sure what, in the long term, the consequences will be; whether, for example, the mechanism by which the culture is carried to successive generations will become less, or more, efficient. What is clear is that changes in the content of social training – the values that are transmitted – are by no means independent of these changes in the techniques of transmission. Indeed, as our dis-cussion has demonstrated, the complex system of social con-ditioning is itself inextricably bound up with a whole range of other learning, and in particular with the acquisition of language skills and modes of thinking and reasoning. It is convenient, for purposes of analysis, to distinguish certain aspects or segments of the socialization process, but it is vital not to lose sight of their essential interdependence.

Some years ago the social anthropologist Margaret Mead wrote: 'The way in which each human infant is transformed into the finished adult, into the complicated individual version of his city and his century, is one of the most fascinating studies open to the curious-minded. Our own generation, conscious of the extent to which the survival of the species hinges upon the moral decisions of men and women, may well regard it as a study of singular practical importance.'[1]

1 Mead, M. *Growing up in New Guinea* (Penguin Books, 1942).

John Bowlby

Security
and Anxiety

A great deal of a psychiatrist's time is spent with people who
are anxious – often intensely anxious – and in trying to help
them feel more secure. Sometimes their anxiety arises in circumstances that would make anyone anxious – after a bereave-
ment or some other calamity – but at other times the reasons
for anxiety are far from obvious. What is more, some people
seem perpetually anxious in contrast to others whom, it
seems at least, nothing affects. How do we understand all
this? What sorts of things make people feel secure and what
sorts make them feel anxious?

As with most of the other big questions in psychiatry and
psychology, there is still no agreement among professionals
about the answers; and here I will give an account of just one
line of research and one line of theorizing.

It began about fifteen years ago. At that time my colleague
James Robertson and I began to tackle this question: why is
it that after a young child has been away from his mother and
family for a few weeks, say in hospital or residential nursery,
he is usually unsettled and anxious? Not only may this
anxiety be intense but sometimes it lasts a long time. Since
those days in the early nineteen-fifties a great many observations of young children have been made both in this country
and abroad; and, in an effort to get more exact results, young
monkeys have also been subjected to a number of experiments. The findings of all these studies are pretty consistent.

The first and most obvious thing is that when a young child
is away from his mother's care and in the hands of strangers
he is upset and frets – which means that he wants to get back

to her. Often he cries or screams, but even when he does not it is clear to a sympathetic observer that much of the day and most of the night there is only one thought in his mind – returning to mother. Many people have found it difficult to believe that even when a child is with kindly people in a good environment he is still unhappy for much of the time and still wants to get back to his family; but I think the evidence is unmistakable.

One of my colleagues, Christoph Heinicke, studied the behaviour of half a dozen children, aged between one and three years, during their first fortnight in a residential nursery; and he contrasted their behaviour with other children (matched for age and background) who were spending their first fortnight at a day nursery. The nursery settings were very much alike, but one lot of children were residents and the other lot just attended during the day. One of the things he recorded was how long the children cried and what about. He found that, throughout the first fourteen days, the residential children cried at least twice as long as the day attenders, and during the second week the difference was extremely marked. Whereas the day children cried for only two or three per cent of the time, the residential children cried about five times as much, that is to say between five and seven minutes in each hour. And for most of that time they were crying for mother. That is a large fraction of a child's day to be crying for his mother – and this was still continuing on the eighteenth day of his stay.

Not only do we know that children of this age are overtly distressed and cry a great deal when they are away from home, but we also know that after they return home – even after what has been by all ordinary standards a benign and kindly experience, and even when they have been away for only two or three weeks – they are scared of it happening again. This was first brought to our attention by some observations which Robertson made on children in a long-stay hospital. He was a regular visitor at the hospital and made good friends with some of the children; he played with them and they got to know him and obviously enjoyed his company. When the children went home he visited them, and he found that one of these children, a little girl of two-and-a-half, was absolutely terrified of him. She ran away, slammed shut the bedroom door, and did everything she could to keep away from him. This was so striking that, in our subsequent work, we set out to be more systematic. For instance, Heinicke made a second study[1] of two-year-old children in a residential nursery; this time he contrasted their behaviour with that of a similar group of children who simply stayed in their own home. On this occasion the observer, who had been observing each child in the nursery setting for the two or three weeks he stayed there, avoided visiting the home until the child had been back there for sixteen weeks. So, after an interval of four months, a person whom the child had seen regularly in the nursery visits him at home. What happens? The children clearly recognize who it is – and all but one immediately withdraw. This behaviour is in sharp contrast to that of the other children in the study who had been observed by the same person but in their own homes. After a sixteen-week interval they too were visited by the observer; all eight made a friendly approach, and none avoided him. The children who had originally been observed during their stay in the residential nursery, and who showed anxiety and withdrew, had only been away from home for two or three weeks. Even so the experience had obviously left its mark; as long as sixteen weeks later these children were more anxious and more apprehensive than they had been before. There is good evidence that what such children are frightened of is a repetition of what they have been through.

There is no doubt that the kinds of experience they have while they are away makes a difference – whether they are treated kindly or not, whether they have been ill, and so on –

but the plain fact is that perfectly ordinary children hate being with strangers in a strange place, even when the strangers are kind, and they long to be at home with mother. With mother they show every sign of feeling secure; separated from her with strangers they show every sign of feeling anxious; after a separation they are anxious lest the experience be repeated. The younger the children the more evident all this is, though in babies of under six months the response is much more puzzling.

A few years ago I reviewed the current ideas on this matter, and it was clear that for some decades one idea had been dominant in intellectual circles. I emphasize 'intellectual circles', because it may well be that plenty of ordinary people thought otherwise — and perhaps thought more wisely. But in psychological and psychiatric circles it had been rather blandly assumed that the reason children become interested in mother is that she feeds them, and the reason they are upset when separated from her is that they are afraid that their unsatisfied desire for food will become unbearably painful. As you probably know, a great deal of psychological theorizing has been built round feeding in infancy. I never thought this fitted the facts because many children who have had an unhappy feeding experience grow up happy and cheerful, whereas other children who have had easy feeding experiences, but whose mothers have not cared for them, turn out the reverse. Nevertheless, a great deal of thinking in academic and clinical circles has been fixated on feeding. It was studies of animals that first called this notion in question; and I think now there is abundant evidence that it is wrong. But what is the alternative?

First, let us remember that it is not only human infants who make a strong attachment to a mother-figure. Many species of bird make it, probably all mammals, and certainly all of man's nearest relatives, the monkeys and apes. When we look at the problem in this broader perspective we get an altogether different picture of it. It was the famous Austrian observer of animal behaviour, Konrad Lorenz, who gave the lead. Through his work with young goslings and ducklings he demonstrated that these young creatures have a strong tendency to follow a mother-figure in spite of the fact that she does not feed them. He also demonstrated that they will follow a man. Then he and others found that they would even follow a cardboard box. In fact, goslings and ducklings have an extremely strong propensity to follow the first moving thing they meet, irrespective of getting any reward.

But what about monkeys and apes, which are so much more closely related to us biologically than birds? The first thing we discover about young monkeys and apes is that they spend the whole of their infancy very close to their mothers, and for much of the time actually clinging to her. They rarely get far from mother, and when they do she pulls them back – often by catching hold of their tails. When she moves off, either she scoops up the infant to help him cling to her, or else he springs to catch hold of her. Either way the two stick together, and any attempt at a forcible separation is met with violent resistance from both parties.

This clinging by young monkeys and apes has its parallel in human young. It has been known for a long time that human infants at birth are able to support their own weight by clinging and that if they are given a rod to hang on to they will cling to that. In the ordinary course of events a human baby is happy to be held and does not cling, but if you start putting him down or even if you move suddenly he at once grabs hold of you. A baby of a few months old often clings pretty hard, and he does so particularly when he is scared. So it is a mistake to suppose that clinging is absent in humans. At one time it was imagined that this clinging of newborn babies is a relic of a time when we inhabited the trees, but a far more probable explanation is that it represents the human version of the clinging to mother that is seen in every one of the other six hundred primate species. And this suggests that much of what we can discover about monkey clinging is likely to be relevant to man.

In recent years there has been a good deal of research into the behaviour of young monkeys. This has shown without the least doubt that a young monkey's strong propensity to cling is there right from the start; it does not develop because he learns that if he does so he will be fed. Actually what happens is just the opposite. A newborn monkey first clings to his mother's belly; he then discovers that there is something in the vicinity of his mouth which can be sucked, and, finally, that when he sucks he comes by food. He discovers the food because he clings to his mother.

Professor Harry Harlow of Wisconsin University has carried this story some way further. First, he showed in a series of experiments that a young monkey will cling to any object, provided it is soft. It does not need to be a real monkey mother – it can be just a dummy – and it does not need to provide food. Secondly, he showed that as he grows older the young monkey uses whatever dummy object he is familiar with as a base from which to explore the world, and as a refuge to run to when he is frightened. Here are two of Harlow's ingenious experiments.[2]

Imagine a large, empty packing-case some six feet on each dimension. Then put in it a few things a young monkey likes to play with. Next bring a young monkey from his familiar cage and put him in the strange box. How does he behave? All he does is lie on the floor and scream, or else curl up and suck his toes. He does not explore and he does not play, and he looks a very miserable little monkey. Yet his whole behaviour is transformed if you do just one thing – put into the box the dummy to which he has been accustomed in his own cage. The dummy is simply a roll of wire with some towelling wound round it. Yet the young monkey's behaviour is transformed. First he clings to the dummy. Then he makes a brief excursion from it and quickly returns. Then he makes a longer excursion and plays with a bit of paper, and so on. So long as the dummy is there he is an active, happy-looking little monkey; once it is removed he reverts to lying curled up on the floor.

In another of Harlow's experiments the young monkey is in his cage with his familiar dummy. Then the experimenter opens the cage and puts into it a little toy animal that moves – say a toy dog that wags its head and its tail. As soon as the little monkey sees this strange object he takes fright and rushes to cling to his familiar dummy. Once there he becomes more relaxed, looks about him and begins to take an interest in the toy dog that had alarmed him so much. After a time he even ventures away from his familiar dummy to investigate the alarming object. But if his familiar dummy is not there he remains in a state of alarm and anxiety until the toy is removed.

In both these experiments the dummy seems to provide the young monkey with a sense of security. Yet the dummy provides no real protection – any more than the toy dog threatens any real danger. I expect you will see the scientific problem this poses. To have a sense of security is one thing; to be safe may be quite another. Similarly, to be frightened is one thing and to be in real danger quite another. Yet a sense of security and being safe are obviously related in some way, just as fright and being in danger are related.

I believe the solution to this problem is not too difficult, but to see it we need to get away from the artificial surroundings of western civilization. We need to think instead of the conditions in which monkeys still live in the wild, and in which humans also lived until not so very long ago. On the one hand, the creatures must obtain sufficient food – which entails moving around to explore – and, on the other hand, they must avoid becoming the prey of animals of other species. The constant presence of predators – wolves and jackals, lions and tigers, eagles and hawks – is one of the great facts of life in

C

the wild, but it is all too easily forgotten in a laboratory or in a modern city. It almost certainly explains much that is otherwise puzzling about the social behaviour of both monkeys and men.

During the last ten years a number of studies have been made of monkeys and apes in the wild.[3] Whatever the species, these animals always live in groups. Some are in small family parties, but the majority live in troops which have a stable membership – usually of from a dozen to fifty animals – and a good deal of social structure. Apart from a few well-grown males of big species, the isolated monkey or ape is absolutely unknown in the wild. De Vore, a student of baboons, points out that every baboon spends the whole of his life within a few feet of another baboon. This means that the bond that ties infant monkey to mother monkey is only one element of a general tendency for monkeys always to remain close to their kin. It is clear that this behaviour has great survival value. So long as the troop sticks together, the prospects of a predator getting a meal are slim. But once an animal becomes isolated, the predator pounces. And a young animal would have no hope of escape. This means that animals who do not develop attachment behaviour are unlikely to leave any offspring while those who do develop it live to breed. In fact there is a strong selection pressure in favour of animals who show a propensity for 'togetherness'.

If this analysis is right, we see the behaviour of human children in a new light. Any form of behaviour that tends to develop in all members of a species and that can be shown to have survival value has traditionally been described as instinctive. The behaviour of a young human child by which he constantly maintains proximity to familiar figures I believe is of this kind. It develops just as surely (or unsurely) as eating behaviour and sexual behaviour, and it has been, until very recent times, just as important for our survival. In fact it is as natural for a child to maintain an attachment to a mother figure as it is for a young man to maintain an attachment to a young woman. Both forms of behaviour have survival value for the species – though in neither case is the individual the least interested in what its survival value may be. What each does is what it is in his nature to do. If successful he feels good; if unsuccessful, frustrated and unhappy.

Near his mother, or at least accessible to her, a child feels secure and has confidence to explore the world and its dangers. Separated from her he feels anxious – he has no familiar base to which to retreat. (And the same is true of grown-ups: at an anxious moment we all feel better for the presence of our relatives or friends.) Studies of this sort raise practical questions: about mothers going out to work, the age when a child should start nursery school, how children should be cared for when ill. As time goes on the best solutions will become clearer. Meanwhile, we are wise to be wary. Any move that separates young children from their mothers needs scrutiny, for we are dealing here with a deep and ancient part of human nature.

REFERENCES

1 Heinicke, C. M. and Westheimer, I. J. *Brief separations* (Longmans, 1966).
2 Foss, B. M., *Determinants of infant behaviour*, Vol. 1 (Methuen, 1961).
3 De Vore, I., ed. *Primate behaviour* (Holt, 1965).

Penelope Leach   # The Rigid Child

Every one of us has been a child and most of us become parents. So we all think that we know something about bringing up children. It sometimes seems, from the advice dealt out in magazines and baby books, as though it is only necessary to adopt a certain practice in order to achieve a specific and desirable result. In fact most of this advice arises out of tradition, mixed with fashion and seasoned with technology. Nobody could know the value of baby-bouncers until somebody invented one! Most of this advice owes very little to scientific research: often it goes against the current research trend.

In the past, research workers did devote themselves to investigating the kind of practice which the baby books still deal with. Scientific attempts to find the optimum times and methods of feeding, weaning and toilet training were made. And many studies attempted to show differences in adults due to differences in these early practices. Most of these attempts failed. If you examine what a mother does in one respect with her infant, you ignore the question of how she does it. This is unsatisfactory: two babies may have been toilet trained at the identical stage in their development, but they may have had very different toilet training experiences. Furthermore, attempts to relate differences in specific aspects of early handling to later personality almost invariably become lost in the complications of time. A traumatic weaning period may indeed effect an individual forever, but so much happens to him between his weaning and his maturity that it is almost impossible to establish the cause and effect relationship.

In recent years a different approach has been taken by most research into child-rearing. This approach starts from the premise that a mother brings to child-rearing the whole complex of her own personality. Everything she does with her children will be within the framework of her own needs, values and attitudes. This approach looks at overall differences between mothers, as people, rather than specific differences in what they do. And it seeks to relate these overall difference in mothers to similarly global differences among their children. We tend therefore to consider a mother's overall democracy or warmth or acceptance of her child, in relation to his later security, independence or creativity, rather than the mother's weaning methods in relation to her child's smoking habits when he is twenty. On the whole this type of work has been very fruitful. It looks at child-rearing in terms of the relationships between the people concerned, rather than in terms of a sort of technology of child-handling. And it produces information which is about real people, rather than about some fictitious average mother or normal child.

One of the global variables which has been studied in children is rigidity. Work on rigidity began with observations showing that certain individuals found it difficult to adapt their responses quickly to changing stimuli. For example, when carrying out a simple repetitive motor task in a laboratory experiment, the subject would continue with his first learned response for a long time after his instructions had been changed so that a second response had become appropriate. Over some years, early in this century, similar types of response were observed in a variety of situations, and some psychologists reached the conclusion that there was an overall syndrome of rigidity, such that the individual who behaved in this perseverative way in one situation would behave similarly in other situations.

Rigidity has therefore been generally defined as 'slowness of response adaptation'. This means that rigid people find it extremely difficult to change or adjust their behaviour quickly to meet different situations. They are happiest, and perform best, with familiar, habitual and predictable events. And they tend to behave as if those events were going on even when they are not; they ignore, or misinterpret the unexpected. Rigid behaviour may extend from the practical to the emotional and inter-personal. Rigid children tend to have stereotyped views of social groups – old people, Negroes, babies and so on – and these will be maintained against a great deal of contrary evidence. They will also tend to adopt extremely conventional attitudes towards their parents and siblings, viewing them as intrinsically good and lovable just because they are blood relatives. Even the way in which such a child approaches ordinary everyday objects may be affected. While we all assume that spoons are for stirring tea and knives for spreading butter, most of us could reverse these functions in an emergency. But the truly rigid child may go without butter on his bread rather than spread it with anything but a knife.

Rigidity is really a pathological exaggeration of normal human behaviour. All human beings select and filter the stimuli which they take from the environment. We have to do this or we could not function at all. If you walked into a room and perceived everything in it, you would be so busy seeing, hearing, smelling, feeling what was in that room that you would have no time to function as a human being at all. In the same way, we have to categorize people and objects, otherwise each person we met, each object we used, would have to be examined at length before we could interact with it. But the rigid person takes this selective perception and categorization to an extreme degree. He goes through life using only a minute part of his environment, refusing to accept, to see, hear or recognize many of the things which go on around him. And unlike the normal person, he does this not in the interests of efficiency, but as a way of defending himself against things which he finds alarming or upsetting in some way.

While some psychologists have studied rigidity as an overall syndrome, there are others who deny its existence as an entity. They maintain that the separate pieces of behaviour which I am calling rigid are psychologically separate, and that they do not add up to an overall pattern of approach to the world. I have recently carried out a piece of research designed to see whether children who did react rigidly to tests in one aspect of their lives, also tended to be rigid in other areas. Finding that this was so, I then went on to see whether extreme rigidity in children was related to being brought up by any particular kind of mother – in the general personality sense which I described earlier.

The tests of rigidity which I used with these eleven-year-old children were designed to cover as wide a range of behaviour as possible: from simple visual perception, to complex moral judgements. One concerned the child's ability to classify ordinary objects on a variety of different bases. A large collection of objects, containing such things as ornaments, cutlery, tinned soup, apples, matches, knitting needles and toys was given to each child. He was asked to sort these into groups in any way he liked. Most children started by grouping them according to function – things to eat, things for playing with, mummy's things. When he had grouped all the objects, I would say: 'yes, that's fine, that's a perfectly good way of sorting them. Now think of a different way.' The point of course was that these objects could also be grouped by more abstract variables, such as their colour or material. But in order to classify them in this way they had to be removed from their functional groups, so that the tin of soup ended up with the knitting wool because both were red, or with the pliers because both were metal. The non-rigid children had no difficulty with this. But the rigid children often could not see any other way to sort the objects. Sometimes they could not even recognize the validity of an abstract grouping when it was presented to them ready assembled. 'But that can't be right' said one. 'The wool must go with mother's things and the apple is for eating . . .' The similarity of colour was simply not recognized.

A further test concerned the children's ability to change their solution to a problem in response to a change in the nature of the problem. A series of simple outline maps in rectangular grid form was presented on a slide viewer. The child had to indicate which was the shortest route through the map from a consistent starting point to a consistent finish. The first five maps all had a single diagonal road across the grid which was *not* a short cut. Children very quickly learned to avoid this road, and to go round the edge of the map to the finish. But the second five maps – otherwise identical with the first – also contained a diagonal, but this time it ran the other way so that it was, in fact, a short-cut. Most of the non-rigid children spotted this reasonably quickly, and changed to using the short-cut. But the rigid children tended not to see it. They had become so set on their chosen route round the map that the possibility of a new and quicker route simply did not occur to them. They could not adjust their response to the change in the problem.

The readiness of the children to take a stereotyped view of people was tested with a series of photographs for which captions had to be chosen out of four alternatives provided for each picture. The captions were carefully written so that for each picture there were two captions which were descriptive of the photograph, and two which were over-generalizations about the picture's subject matter, and positively untrue in relation to that picture. One photograph, for example, was of a small baby, sound asleep in its cot cuddling a toy duck. The over-generalized captions were 'Babies do nothing but cry' which was clearly inaccurate as this particular baby wasn't crying; and 'Baby girls are prettier than baby boys' which was idiotic since this picture gave no sex indication. Many rigid children selected this kind of caption, though non-rigid children tended to choose instead 'This baby likes his duck' (a reasonable assumption) and 'Sleeping soundly' which was obviously true.

A final example should suffice to demonstrate the breadth of these rigid responses. The children were given a test of moral judgements which consisted of a set of eight rules which pilot work had shown to be general in the lives of all these children. Each of the rules was printed facing a cartoon picture of a child of similar age to the subjects who was breaking the rule for a socially acceptable reason. For example, the rule 'You must never speak to strangers in the street' faced a picture of an old lady who had fallen in the street and spilt her shopping bag. A girl had stopped and was saying to her, 'I say are you all right? Can I help you up?' The rigid children would respond with 'Oh! she's wrong. You mustn't. No you mustn't ever speak to strangers. It's a rule.' The non-rigid children would say 'Yes, of course that's all right. The rule is about going with people, or taking sweets and things from people who might do you harm. This old lady needs help and it's only polite to speak to her.' The rigid children could only stick to the letter of the law, whereas the non-rigid children could accept the meaning behind the rule, and therefore balance it against other kinds of desirable behaviour.

Rigid children seem to live on tramlines in a black and white world. There are no sidetracks and no shades of grey. Things are what they are; right is always right and wrong wrong. Rules are to be kept and not questioned. All these things are certainties, and a great deal of their energy goes into maintaining this certainty. For underneath their usually placid, conforming exteriors, uncertainty, ambiguity, choice, are the things they most fear.

What makes such a child so different from most of us? The answer lies in his fear. While we all use the oversimplifying mechanisms these tests measure, most of us use them to make us more efficient in managing our extremely complex environment. And when the facts do not fit our presumptions, we are most of us quick to revise them. But the rigid child needs his preconceived ideas about the world. They are vital to his defence against the fear of ambiguity. So when situations do not fit the ideas, it is the situations which must be changed, or ignored, or misperceived; the rigid ideas must be kept intact.

Like so many other things in later life, this fear of uncertainty, this need to have everything black and white, predictable and clear-cut, seems to go back to early infancy. All babies turn from being completely egocentric beings – concerned only for their own gratification – into social beings, largely through their affectionate tie with the mother or her permanent substitute. Very gradually babies find that certain pieces of their own behaviour please the mother, and that her pleasure makes things nicer for them. It is still their own pleasure which is the issue, but the interaction between their own and another person's pleasure begins to impinge.

There comes a time when a mother begins to make actual demands for certain kinds of behaviour, rather than simply being delighted when they occur spontaneously. When she does this, she puts an apparent price on her love for the baby. The fact that she loves him in an overall way, which is quite unaffected by the minutiae of daily life, cannot impinge on him yet. As far as he is concerned, her feelings for him are demonstrated only in her actions moment by moment.

If this apparent price on the mother's love is too high, the baby is in a truly desperate position. The price may be too high if he simply cannot understand what is wanted of him and therefore cannot be right whatever he does. Or it may be too high if he can understand, but is simply not mature enough to perform what is wanted. He may lack physiological maturity, or he may lack memory; he may be quite unable to keep in his mind some injunction, even though he fully understands it. Or he may understand, and have the necessary maturity, but his own desire to do the forbidden thing may be so great that he is between the Scylla of his mother's (and therefore his own) displeasure, and the Charybdis of non-performance. If, for any of these reasons, the child cannot fulfil his mother's expectations completely, then he will try to do so in part, and this is where rigidity may begin.

Consider the mother who is trying to teach her toddler to be clean. The concept as a whole is, of course, meaningless to him. It consists of a series of apparently unrelated whims. Mother would rather he used the pot than his pants. She doesn't like sand on the kitchen floor, but curiously enough she minds this much more if she's just been playing with her bucket of soapy water. She likes him to spread finger paint on paper, but not shepherd's pie on his table. She objects to mud on his clothes, but not to carrots on his bib. This mother may not only fail to be pleased when things are done wrong, she may be positively cross. Using your pot is good, using your pants is bad. The toddler is bewildered, but since his own happiness is dependent on his mother's, he is, by definition anxious to please. So he does the best he can. He learns, one at a time and piecemeal, the things his mother does and does not like him to do. He is learning nothing about hygiene, but he is learning how to steer his way through the day without trouble. He learns about the pot, and because it matters so much to his mother, and therefore to him, he pushes away his desire to play with and welcome his excretions. He accepts, without understanding, that this is different from sand, or clay. This is the child who four years later may suffer torments, and ruin the family outing, because he cannot relieve himself behind a hedge. He learns also to keep his clothes clean, and again may become the nursery school child who cannot paint or play with plasticine.

As children grow up they themselves take over, and take into themselves, the teaching and discipline of the mother. Her commands and wishes are internalized so that eventually teeth are brushed not because she sees to it but because the child knows himself that this is desirable. General principles of behaviour have been established and as the child goes into school, away from the mother's immediate and constant influence, these principles tell him how to behave in new circumstances on which he has had no specific teaching. But the poor anxious rigid toddler has never had the time or the peaceful calm to discover the general principles behind his mother's teaching. His piecemeal learning has become a habit. He has never learnt hygiene, but only the wrongness of excreting anywhere but in a lavatory. And the dichotomized, learnt minutiae of right and wrong tend to be applied by this child not only to his behaviour in relation to other people, but in relation to himself and his own feelings too.

This kind of upbringing must, by its nature, by its apparent total injustice, make a toddler bitterly angry and sad. Angry at the frustration of natural wishes; sad at the loss of his mother's affection when he cannot see how or where he has gone wrong. The rage and the misery are almost intolerable to the child. Anyone who has ever seen a two-year-old temper tantrum must realize that the emotion felt is overwhelming. And anyone who has nursed such a child through the shaking pallid aftermath, knows the terror which such an excess of emotion can arouse in him. All this anger, all this sadness, has to be suppressed if the mother's love is to be successfully retained. Not only must the sand not go on the floor, when immature muscles cannot keep it in its bucket, but the frustration aroused must be given no outlet. The child feels 'I hate you' but he must say 'yes mummy' or even 'I'm sorry'. The only way the anger can be covered up is by an excess of good feeling. 'I love you' must replace 'I hate you'. So rigid children tend to express a stereotyped and exaggerated love and affection for their parents. They dare not do otherwise. To admit to the slightest criticism of these controlling figures would be to risk opening the floodgates of that long forgotten, childish, uncomprehending and terrifying rage.

This kind of insensitivity to the needs and feelings of infants appears to go with a personality syndrome which we call authoritarianism. Authoritarian mothers are no more likely than any other mothers to be neglectful, rejecting or cruel. Like the vast majority of parents, they do what they consider to be the best for their children. But authoritarian adults have a rather particular approach to the social world, and, of course, the social world includes their own children. The authoritarian mother lives in a highly structured social world. The structure is based on considerations of power, of strength, of in-groups and out-groups. It is a black and white picture. White is the mores of her own social group or the one she aspires to. Black is everybody and everything else. One of the manifestations of this is, of course, prejudice; anti-semitic, anti-foreign, anti-Negro prejudice. All these tend to go with authoritarianism.

The mother whose personality is highly authoritarian, and who therefore rejects everything that is different from her, or from what she would like to be, tends to see her children as something very separate from herself. Their behaviour contravenes her own extreme conventionality. Their ignorance of what is socially right or wrong continually threatens her with embarrassment. And since, for such a woman, all social relationships involve power – leading, or following, being superior or inferior to someone – she tends to see her children as clearly her inferiors. The children must be moulded, in a deliberate way, to be as like her as possible, as quickly as possible. She tends to feel that she must teach them how to behave, rather than teaching them how to make their own space without impinging on the space of other people. One such mother said to me, quite kindly: 'In bringing up children, obedience is the first essential. I'm older than the children. They must learn to respect what I say; this is the only way I can save them from the world.' This is not, to me, like one human being talking about another. It is like somebody leading a pet dog of low intelligence through a particularly dangerous jungle. Another mother, from a low authoritarian group could find only this to say: 'I don't know what I do. We rub along. Sometimes one of us is cross, sometimes we're all cheerful. I just take it easy and it seems to work.'

In my research it was the rigid children, as distinguished by these tests, who had the highly authoritarian mothers, as distinguished by accepted measures. But of course it can be argued that the rigidity tests used were a far cry from reality; that the children's performance on the tests did not reflect their ordinary behaviour. Such an argument only tends to support the case for a relationship between authoritarian upbringing and later rigidity. The point about the rigidity tests was that they were so designed that no child could have been taught how to perform on them. If one interviews the children of highly authoritarian parents, and asks them about such things as ethnic prejudice, one almost always finds that the children echo the parents' attitudes. They have heard these things discussed at home, and they have picked up the parental viewpoint. This tells one more about the parents than about the children. But rigidity is not something which children have heard discussed at home. It is not a concept of which most parents have heard. Therefore rigid reactions from children, to test material outside the context of normal everyday life, is the more telling. John Smith may tell me that all Negroes are lazy, because that is what daddy says. But daddy did not tell him what to do if somebody asked him to find the shortest route through a lot of maps.

In child-rearing research, it is usually impossible to make a rational judgement as to what kind of upbringing is or is not desirable. Usually we are so unsure what kind of adult we are trying, as a society, to produce, that we are in no position to attempt blueprints. But in this area many people would accept that rigidity is an unfortunate tendency, simply because it restricts the use a child can make of his environment, and therefore restricts his own use of his potential. But even if this value-judgement is made, what can be done about it? As with most ills, prevention is very much easier than cure. And even here there are difficulties. Children have to be brought up. They have to be told what to do and often they have to be prevented from doing what they want. So what can be done to avoid the black picture I have painted?

Nothing, so far as we know, can be done, outside psycho-analysis, to change the highly authoritarian personality. These extreme parents will continue to take the attitude I have described to their children. But many of us take unwittingly authoritarian attitudes to our own children when these are not basic to our own personalities: out of laziness or lack of thought, rather than out of unconscious psychopathology. If we can think better about our own child-rearing, fewer children with rigid tendencies will be produced. Our children may therefore, in their turn, do better by the next generation.

Perhaps the most important thing to remember is that a baby's own happiness is vested in his mother's pleasure in him. To imagine that he wishes to displease is to imagine that he wants to make himself unhappy. He doesn't 'do it to annoy because he knows it teases'. He does it because he wants to, or needs to; or he wants and needs to know what will happen if he does. What may happen is that his mother is cross. There is no harm in this. But given that these quarrels are all experi-mental and that, by definition, there is no malice in a depen-dent child, all the power lies with the mother, and she can afford to use it gently. Does it really matter if the child does the forbidden thing? Is it the action, or the sensation of being vanquished to which the mother is reacting? If it is genuinely the first, what alternative can she provide?

This question of alternatives is vitally important. If children must not play with the contents of their pots, what else, of similar delicious colour and texture, can they play with? At least this approach enables us to put the demands positively rather than negatively: explore this, rather than simply, don't touch that.

At the same time, where demands must be made before the child is able to understand the reasons behind them, at least we can avoid giving the demands moral overtones. If the child is too young to prefer a clean kitchen floor to a sandy one, why do we find it so difficult to ask him to keep the sand in the sand pit *because we prefer it*? Why is it so much easier to maintain that it's naughty to put it on the floor? If the child knows his mother dislikes sand in the house, her irritation when it gets there will at least be comprehensible; whereas at this stage 'You are a naughty boy' can only be mysteriously anxious-making. If the idea of 'naughtiness' can be kept separate from tiresomeness, the child will find it far easier to come to terms with the adult view of morality.

With these attempts to adjust demands to children's understanding, and to avoid lending moral weight to requests which are only for our own convenience, it is also important to guard against giving a child rigid ideas simply because they are easy to communicate and enforce. Children have to be prevented from burning themselves. The easiest way to do this is to put up fireguards and teach them never to touch fires. But this is too easy. Children see us touching fires, switching them on, lighting them, poking them. Furthermore eventually they will touch an unlit electric fire and find it cold and their parents irrational. Surely we have to take the trouble to teach them that fires that are on, or lit, are hot and will burn *if carelessly handled*. It is more complicated, but at least it is true.

In moral behaviour adults can be even more confusing. Most of us accept that there are no moral absolutes; that all behaviour can be judged only by circumstance and motive. Yet just as we tend to teach children not to touch fires, so we tend to give them rules for behaviour as if they were absolutes. One mother told me that 'If you start children off on the straight and narrow path they will never leave it; all they need are the rules to show them the way.' That path led straight to rigidity of thought. Such a mother is trying to be a sort of remote control guidance system for her child, instead of seeing that he has his own inbuilt controls, and then contenting herself with the role of launching pad. If a mother tries to tell her child what to do in all circumstances, she will fail. She is not going to foresee everything her child will meet with, and anyway behaviour which would be right for her, will not always be right for him. He is a different person. General principles of behaviour, of respect for other people, are all she can hope to give him. Principles which will enable him to be the judge of whether this is an old lady who needs help with her spilt shopping, or a personal threat in the shape of a stranger in the street.

If he can judge this for himself, and act on his judgement, then he is at least not rigid. For this is what the rigid child cannot do. He cannot judge for himself because he cannot let himself be himself. That self is still caught up somewhere way back in the bewildered toddler. So, looking at the old lady on the pavement, he does not consider the situation; that would be to admit an intolerable uncertainty. There is safety only in the rule: 'You mustn't talk to strangers in the street. . . .'

D

Colin Hindley

Ability and Social Class

Since the pioneering work of Sir Cyril Burt, and others, it has been known that the ability of school children – and adults for that matter – is related to social class. So, on the average, children of professional and middle-class parents score higher on intelligence tests than children of manual workers. And whatever method we may use to select children for secondary education, the chances of children of manual workers getting into a secondary grammar school, or grammar stream in comprehensive schools, are substantially less than those of children of middle-class parents.

Several investigations have demonstrated that these social-class differences in ability increase, rather than diminish, as children become older,[1] and the Robbins report showed that social class is a big factor in getting a place in a university. The recognition not only that we need many more well-educated people, but that a great deal of potential ability is being wasted, has led to the recent efforts to improve our secondary schools, largely by making them comprehensive, and to an expansion of university and technical college facilities.

In contrast, ever since the end of the Second World War, there has been little change in the facilities available at the other end of the educational process – namely, at the pre-school stage. In fact, there are only 460 local authority nursery schools, with 30,000 places, in the whole country. Is this a wise way to apportion our educational resources? If the difference in abilities between children of different social classes increases, when does this process begin? Has it already begun before children begin compulsory schooling at the age of five?

I want to describe some research which throws an interesting light on this question, though – as is often the case in research work – it also raises a number of other questions for further investigation. These results come from one aspect of the longitudinal research project at the Centre for the Study of Human Development of the University of London Institute of Education.

A longitudinal study is one in which the same children are seen repeatedly at regular intervals, so that it becomes possible to see how the individual changes during his development. Attempts to record rather comprehensively the psychological development of samples of children first began in the USA over thirty years ago. However, in Britain, although there have been longitudinal studies of limited aspects of development, and one or two wider follow-ups by survey methods, ours is the only comprehensive longitudinal study on a sample of normal children from birth to maturity. It began with over 200 expectant mothers, living in central London, and we have been able to record the development of their children from early babyhood to their present ages – which are between thirteen and fifteen years.

Our sample contains children of widely differing social class backgrounds, and, although it is not large by survey standards, we have been able – through the International Children's Centre – to compare our findings with those of four other European studies which are using similar methods, and rather less directly with other studies in more remote parts of the world. The methods we have used have included regular interviews with mothers about the home background, about the child's behaviour, and about the parents' methods in bringing up their child. We have seen the child himself at equally regular intervals, and have studied his characteristics by a variety of methods, including tests of both abilities and personality, observation of play, and reports from schools.

To assess their abilities in the pre-school years, all the children were tested at six months and eighteen months with the Griffiths Scale, a test of infant development; and at three years and five years with the well-known Stanford–Binet intelligence test. The Griffiths Scale gives an approximate measure of the level of maturity which an infant has reached in his behaviour. The standard is what the average child of his age can do. There are several different aspects here. Take locomotion, for instance: landmarks which are looked for are: whether he can roll over, sit without support, make stepping movements when he is held – and at later stages, whether he can crawl, or walk.

Then there are hearing and speech. We can test hearing, at the earlier stages, by seeing whether the baby will pay attention when a bell is rung, and, a little later, whether he will actively search for the source of the sound. Round about the end of the first year he will probably begin to show signs of understanding the meaning of words. At first he will simply react to 'no', or to his own name. But in the second year we test his understanding of words by asking him to pick out named objects – such as a 'spoon' or 'pussy'. We can evaluate his own use of speech, in the early months, by seeing whether he coos or babbles; and, a little later, whether the babble is of two or three, or four syllables. Once he has begun to use meaningful words, such as 'mama' or 'dada', we can test his vocabulary by getting him to name simple objects and pictures.

Manipulating objects is another ability which develops gradually. At first we test whether he will clutch at a wooden ring, and, a little later, grasp it and manipulate it; or whether he can hold first one cube, and then two or more; and at a later stage whether he can put simple wooden shapes into the right hole in a board.

A young baby's social behaviour is assessed by watching whether he reacts positively to people, first by smiling, and then by more general excitement. Later he will wave goodbye, and play simple repetitive games like clapping hands. We also note his ability to do things for himself, like using a cup or spoon, trying to turn a door knob, taking off his shoes and socks.

So, in assessing the child's level of development a wide range of his behaviour is sampled. Naturally, some children will be more advanced in one direction than another – some in locomotion, others perhaps in speech – but the child's overall score, or developmental quotient (D.Q.) summarizes the average level of development of his various abilities.

On the other hand, the Stanford–Binet test – which we use at three and five years – begins to look more like what we usually think of as an intelligence test. The items involve simple reasoning, such as analogies or a comparison of likenesses and differences. Many of them test the child's general knowledge of his environment; for example, naming objects, or knowing simple properties of them – such as that a cow gives us milk; and most of the items depend on understanding and using speech.

Conducting these tests is not always easy. The children can be fractious or tired, and so may not perform to the best of their ability. This could give misleading results, and so we removed from consideration any children who were not reasonably co-operative on any tests. This left us with eighty children who were satisfactorily tested all four times – that is, at six months, eighteen months, three years, and five years.

In comparing children according to social-class background several criteria can be used, such as father's or mother's occupation, education, or the material standards of their home. In the event, father's occupation provided the most effective measure, and enabled us to divide the sample into three groups.

Using this criterion of social class, our rather small sample gave us two clear results.[2] Firstly, on the test of infant development at six months and eighteen months, there were no significant differences in the average scores of the three social-class groups. All three groups scored round about the average of 100. Secondly, on the intelligence test at three years and five years there were highly significant social class differences in I.Q. Put in another way: if a child's level of ability in relation to that of other children of his age remains constant, his D.Q. and I.Q. will remain constant. This is what happens in our intermediate group, but we find that children from the higher social-class groups show – on the average – a gain in I.Q., and those in the lower groups show a fall. These differences are quite large. While the groups are roughly equivalent at eighteen months, by five years the middle-class children will have gained, on average, seventeen I.Q. points, and children of semi-skilled and unskilled workers will have lost about ten points, as compared with their scores on the infant-tests.

These are the essential findings. Admittedly the sample is small, and one would not wish to generalize too widely from it if it were not for the fact that colleagues in collaborating investigations in Stockholm and Brussels, have since obtained similar results. The results are also consistent in a general way with the findings of several American studies.

What interpretation are we to put on these facts? It is possible to make sense of the data from either the hereditarian or the environmentalist point of view.

The hereditarian can argue that the well-known social-class differences of intelligence in the adult population will lead to children tending to inherit a level of intelligence similar to their parents. As intelligence reveals itself increasingly as children grow older, so the social-class differences in scores will increase with age. We can hardly deny that heredity is an important factor in determining a child's level of intelligence. The weight of evidence is too great. For instance, Honzik,[3] in America, has found that the degree of association between a foster child's I.Q. and that of his true mother (from whom he was separated) increased as he grew older. By the age of six or seven years, the association was quite substantial.

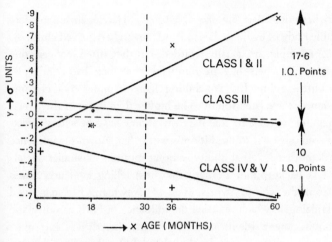

×   classes I & II (Means)

●   classes III (Means)

+   classes IV & V (Means)

(After Hindley and Simpson, unpublished)

Relative abilities of three social class groups from 6 to 60 months.

Diagram shows relative level of ability from six months to sixty months of three social-class groups: I and II, III, IV and V of the Registrar General's Classification of Occupations. The average score of the whole sample at each age is represented by the dotted line at 0. The units (σ units) simply show the degree of departure, upwards or downwards, from the average. There is little difference in the scores at six months and eighteen months on the baby-test, but marked differences on the intelligence test at five years.

On the other hand the correlation between his I.Q. and that of his foster-parents showed only a small rise – and in any case it was not very large at any age.

But the environmentalist can also argue that the reasons for the diverging levels of ability are obvious. Children of more educated parents receive more stimulation to explore and understand their world, and they are exposed to a much richer vocabulary and use of language. Here again a considerable body of evidence lies to hand. Severely deprived children, for example, are usually retarded, but they often recover considerably when they are removed from their bad conditions of life – and the I.Q.s of children fostered under good circumstances have been found to be higher than those of their own parents, suggesting that the foster-home has a beneficial effect. From our own study, Moore's work[4] has shown the influence of mothers' verbal ability, among mothers of similar social-class background. Perhaps the most telling evidence comes from the classic twin-studies of Newman, Freeman, and Holzinger[5] which revealed the influence of both heredity and environment. Identical twins – whose heredity is extremely similar – have more closely related I.Q.s than non-identical twins, who are no more alike in inheritance than ordinary brothers and sisters. But, on the other hand, identical twins who have lived apart for much of their lives may show large differences in I.Q. So it is clear that both factors are at work.

Our study gives us no direct evidence about hereditary factors, but we do have evidence which suggests an environmental influence. We find a significant tendency for children who have a younger brother or sister born within the first five years to fall in I.Q., whereas those who have not tend to rise. However, we do not yet know whether these differences continue beyond five years. The fall in the I.Q. of children with a younger sibling is not simply due to the influence of family size, because it does not appear in relation to whether or not a child has older brothers and sisters.

There are two likely reasons for this fall. First, that the older child will inevitably receive rather less of his mother's attention, and therefore receive less stimulation from her, in his activities and talking. And, secondly, that he may be emotionally affected because he is no longer his mother's primary concern, and may have less keenness to explore his environment.

Leaving this matter of interpretation aside, and assuming that these social-class differences in ability in the pre-school years are real, whatever their cause, let us go back to the issues I raised at the beginning. What are the educational implications of these findings?

In the first place they show that social inequalities begin very early; they are already present to a substantial degree by the time children start school. If we accept that environmental factors are at least partly responsible, this implies that a good deal of potential ability is not being adequately fostered in the pre-school period – and we know from other work that school does not compensate for earlier deficiencies. Indeed, if anything, the differences increase during school life, so the provision of better educational facilities at later ages is not an adequate answer. It seems very much as though the five-year-old child has already – in favourable circumstances – acquired a general knowledge, a set of skills in language and in comprehension, and an approach to the outer world, which will help him in his school work; in unfavourable circumstances he will be handicapped by the lack of these assets.

If we want to counteract this process, it is clear we must do so early – in fact before primary school. This has already been recognized in Israel. There they have a similar problem in that children from homes with an oriental background are already, by the age of five, well behind those from a European background. Oriental culture does not generally encourage free expression in young children, either in speech or in action, so that the child is less likely to acquire exploratory attitudes and less likely to have gained knowledge of the world, and how it works, from his parents. The studies by Bernstein[6] and others suggest that the same is often true here, when we compare working-class and middle-class homes.

In an attempt to remedy this situation, the Israelis have started a programme of pre-school education for the children of oriental parents, in which they lay stress on encouraging speech, and the development of the child's own initiative in exploring and understanding his environment. In America, too, similar work is being done with the children of socially depressed families, and efforts are also being made there to help the parents help their own children.

So far as this country is concerned, a very strong case can be made for a big expansion in nursery-school education, primarily for those children who at the moment are least likely to receive it. This has been recognized to a considerable extent by the Plowden Committee, but if nursery education is to be effective we must recognize the need of young children for a great deal of individual attention, and this means a high ratio of well-trained staff to children.

In terms of immediate cash returns there is little doubt that new technical colleges and universities have great appeal to politicians and administrators. From the point of view of long-term investment, to say nothing of the personal development of the individual, the evidence is becoming increasingly compelling that we can no longer afford to neglect the early years. As things stand now, a sizeable proportion of children simply lose interest in their secondary education, and at that stage it may be too late to do much about it. They are the end-result of a process of educational maladjustment which began much earlier, and our researches suggest that the remedy lies in making much earlier efforts to help these children. In any case, it would be as well for both educators and administrators to recognize that although five years may be the beginning of compulsory schooling, it is by no means the beginning of education.

REFERENCES

1 Douglas, J. W. B. *The home and the school* (MacGibbon and Kee, 1964).
2 Hindley, C. B. 'Stability and change in abilities up to five years' in *The Journal of Child Psychology and Psychiatry*, Vol. 6, 1965. pp. 85–99.

3 Honzik, M. P. 'Developmental studies of parent-child resemblance in intelligence' in *Child Development*, Vol. 28, No. 2, 1957. pp. 215–28.

4 Moore, T. 'Language and intelligence: a longitudinal study of the first eight years' in *Human Development*, Vol. 10, No. 2, 1967, pp. 88–106, and Vol. 11, No. 1, 1968, pp. 1–24 (Basle: S. Karger).

5 Newman, H. H. *and others. Twins: a study of heredity and environment* (University of Chicago Press, 1937).

6 Bernstein, see chapter 5.

Basil Bernstein
in conversation with
David Edge

The Rôle of Language

Dr Bernstein, you have been particularly studying the rôle of language in the socialization process, but is it in fact possible to disengage language from the social structure?

Yes; you have only to consider the language used in the army when a man is on combat duty and then consider the speech the same individual will produce at a padre's evening to realize the effect of the social structure upon what is said.

I gather you distinguish between two sorts of linguistic code: the restricted code and the elaborated code? As I understand it, the restricted code is one that is on the whole predictable, that is relatively concrete and condensed, and is determined by a situation in which there is a good deal of social rigidity, protocol, ritual, and so on. Would this be a fair summary?

I think you have to distinguish between types of restricted code. There is one similar to your suggestion, and that is where all the words in the message are totally predictable. This code is often used, for example, at cocktail parties. If you are meeting someone in a train on a long journey and you are opening the conversation, it is likely that you use this form. It is also found in church, where often large sections of the service are composed of language which is totally predictable. The other type of restricted code is one where you cannot predict the vocabulary. You know that it will be drawn from a narrow range but the syntax that is used is much more capable of prediction than in the case of an elaborated code. In the case of an elaborated code, it is not possible to predict the syntactical alternatives which individuals take up at certain choice points in the language, as easily as you can in the case of a restricted code.

As I understand it the restricted code is bound up with questions of status; it is used in situations where people 'know their place' and know how to interact within a structure which is determined outside the language.

I think this is reasonable. If you know somebody extremely well, if you share a great deal with them, then there is no need to put into words all your meanings; whereas in a situation where you cannot take for granted the intent of the other person, you are forced to expand your meanings verbally and elaborate them.

I would like to quote a sentence that I read from one of your papers: 'The major function of this code [that is the restricted code] is to define and reinforce the form of the social relationship by restricting the verbal signalling of individual experience.' In other words, the restricted code is one in which individuals are, as it were, devalued in the communication?

I think I would prefer to put it this way: that the form of the social relationship can act selectively on the channel which is used by means of which individuals signal their difference. I remember when I was in the Air Force I had to guard a particular place, even though there was nothing there to guard. I placed all the guards except one man in a little hut. Eventually this man ran into the hut wildly and said something which I did not catch, and all the men dashed out, got on parade, and stood with their guns in a particular position. A man came across who was obviously terribly important, and waited. I said the first thing I could think of, which was 'Shoulder arms', and they all did something with their guns and rested them against their shoulders. Then there was a dreadful air of expectation, and I simply did not know what to say. Anyway I went 'wumff, wumff', and they all made the next movement, which obviously was what the important man was expecting. Here one has a situation where the words themselves have little meaning; what is important is the context of the situation. Given the context, then a particular kind of intonation pattern will do the trick. If a person wishes to signal his difference to others, he cannot do it by messing about with the language: the only way in which he can do it is extra-verbally. It is how you say 'wumff, wumff' that counts.

The point I was trying to get at a little earlier is that someone who uses an elaborated code develops particularly the concept of self, through the use of this language.

I would rather qualify it by saying that certain aspects of the self are verbally available to you. That is, that the self is available for verbal exploration if you have an elaborated code. The self is less available for verbal exploration if the person is limited to a particular kind of restricted code, because questions of an individual's intent are not so relevant for verbalization in the social relationship which in fact produces the code. In one case an individual has language in order to explore himself and in another case this question of exploring self is not so relevant for the person; there is less need to do it.

But the fact that he has this verbally available to him surely affects the quality of experience, and the kind of way he structures the raw experience itself. I am thinking particularly in this case of religious language: as you said, ritualistic language is used a good deal in services and so on, but theological language actually makes experiences significant in a special way.

Again I would like to qualify this. There are certain kinds of theologies which place an emphasis upon individual intent, and the consciousness of individual intent, and in these theologies individuals will in fact be invited and compelled to explore their inner experience; but this is not the case with all theologies. One can make the distinction perhaps between an elaborated code which is useful for making relationships between objects, and an elaborated code which is useful for making relationships between persons; so it deals very much with questions of intent, with motivation and social dispositions, and individuals may vary in terms of their control over these codes.

Are you saying that the people who are using an elaborated code on objects have not got the elaborated code centred on persons available to them?

It may well be that if one looks at the original social relationship from which a code is produced, questions of motivation, of disposition, of attitude, of intent, are not relevant in the original social relation, and this whole area so obviously felt in experience is perhaps not raised to the level of verbal elaboration and made explicit. Presumably also the relationships between people are different, the rôles which they learn are different; this might perhaps underlie some of the so-called problems of the 'two cultures'.

In the case of the two cultures, the thesis is that a person who has the one elaborated code towards objects cannot share in the other one. This is why there is the two-cultures split, as it is called. But is it not true that everybody uses both restricted and elaborated codes in the course of life?

If a person has that experience in the rôle and thereby has learned the code, he will be able clearly to switch codes according to social context; but if the range of rôles that individuals have learned has been very narrow, they will not have learned other codes which are necessary and appropriate to the rôles that they are playing in different social contexts.

But an individual can learn the range of codes if he is in the right learning situations at the right time?

I see no reason why not. Presumably the level at which he can operate a code, and the imagination which he uses to develop it, has some basis in his original capacities; but in principle I see no reason why individuals cannot learn a range of codes. The restriction on the range of codes people have is much more related to the social milieu in which they have been brought up. One could conceive a situation where a person has an elaborated code which he can *write*, but he cannot manage the rôle relationships which go with it. So that if in fact you *talk* to him in a context which requires an elaborated code you might find that he could not produce it. This is often the case with certain bright young working-class boys who can write an elaborated code but have much more difficulty in producing it verbally because they have to manage a rôle relation, a relationship between people, which is very different from the one which they have experienced in their own family and community.

Is it too simple to say that, in general, working-class people would use restricted codes and middle-class people elaborated codes?

I think this is much too simple. There is a much higher probability in the working class of finding young children and families who are limited to a restricted code of syntactic prediction, than is the case in the middle class. Certainly one would not want to say that the lower working class are limited to a restricted code, but just that the probability of them being so is much greater than in the middle class. For the middle-class child, who is in a social relationship within the family which moves him in the direction of the elaborated code, the whole school experience is one of social and symbolic development; for the lower-working-class child the school experience is a situation of symbolic and social change, and this is a vastly different experience; within the school, a change of code for this child may mean a change in the very means whereby he creates his reality and relates to individuals.

It is often assumed that the middle-class norm – at least it likes to think of itself as the middle-class norm – of an elaborated code which is person-centred is necessarily a desirable thing in socialization. Would you say that it is a goal which has no dangers?

I think there are great dangers. It has been suggested that the middle class use methods of control which involve loss of love (appeals to guilt, isolation, and reasoning) whereas working-class parents are often initially highly indulgent and are more likely to use coercive methods. But possibly a more interesting distinction has been made by a researcher called Kohn. His research showed that middle-class mothers are more likely to be concerned with why the child acted as he did, more concerned with the child's motivation, whereas working-class mothers are more likely to be concerned with the consequences of the child's act. The working-class mother, then, is more concerned with trying to prevent disobedience and trying to inhibit unrequired behaviour in the child, and here, presumably, there is less 'talking through' of acts, and less verbal investigation of motive. The middle-class mother, it is suggested, will attempt to control the child by the verbal manipulation of the child's feelings, and perhaps by giving reasons which link the child to the significance of his own acts as these relate to him as consequences. So Kohn's researches suggest that the working-class mother is less concerned with the verbalizing of the child's intent and more concerned with the consequences of the child's act: is more likely simply to announce the rule and leave it at that: 'I've told you don't take it – now will you leave it alone.' 'Come over here before I lose my temper – you know that's wrong.' Clearly the middle-class mother when she is cross will do the same – she would be a fool if she didn't. But she is also more likely to explain the rule and put it into a personal context.

An example might help to bring out this distinction. Imagine the situation where a child has to visit his grandfather who is unwell, and the child does not like to kiss him because he has not shaved for a long time. One mother says before the visit: 'You kiss grandpa. I don't want none of your nonsense.' The other mother says: 'I know you don't like to kiss grandpa, but he's very fond of you and it makes him happy.' This second example from one point of view is sheer blackmail. But note that the child's intent is recognized by the mother and linked to the wishes of another. Further, in this second example, there is the appearance of the child having a choice. The mother, so to speak, lays out the situation for the child and the rule is learned in an individualized, interpersonal context. The rule is, so to speak, *achieved* by the child. The child spontaneously, given the situation, opts for the rule. In the first example, where the mother says 'You kiss grandpa, I don't want none of your nonsense', the rule is simply *assigned* in a relationship which relies on latent power for its effectiveness. Because if the child says 'No' here, the mother is quite likely to find other than verbal means of encouraging him to do it. We could call the form of control where rules are achieved, *personal*, and where the rules are assigned, *positional*.

It is clear that where control is personal, whole orders of learning are made available to the child which are not there if the control is positional. Where control is positional, learning about objects, events, and persons is reduced, and the child learns to expect in this relationship that power is going to be used to make him do what is wanted. So the difference between social-class groups is not necessarily difference in the type of rules transmitted but in the manner in which they are transmitted, and this can have a number of consequences. If one thinks about social control in the classroom, control may be difficult because the teacher may move naturally towards a personal control system in a situation where children equally naturally move towards positional control type. Clearly there are certain problems that can arise if the control is personal; the child's world is constantly dissolving into complex meanings which he then has to control and order, and it is likely that, if he does not have a strong trust relationship with his mother, this sort of instability in a constantly changing world can have possibly deleterious consequences.

What you are saying is that personal control can overload the child, the system.

Certainly; and it can also create guilt and anxiety and involve the child with the mother in a way in which the other does not. It may be much easier to rebel where you have a positional system, because the authority is clear-cut, whereas in a personal control process everybody, so to speak, is mixed up with each other, and this means that middle-class children possibly have a much more complicated relationship with their parents than working-class children. Perhaps I should re-phrase this: the kind of complication is different. Where you have positional control, as soon as you challenge it you are challenging the right of the person – the right of the mother or her delegate – to issue this request; as soon as you challenge this you are challenging the whole normative order from which this person derives his right. Whereas where you have personal control this is not the case, because you do not get this challenge of the right of the person either until much later in the relationship or perhaps not at all. Where personal control procedures are used, the basis of control lies in linguist-ically elaborated meanings. Here the rule is personalized and freed from a given context. This may lead to a situation where the child attains autonomy though his identity is *not* refracted back to him by the status arrangements of a social group. This, perhaps, may lead to disturbances in some children, or over-conformity. In the case of positional control procedures, the basis of control lies more in the difference between the formal status of the regulator and regulated. Here the child's identity *is* refracted back to him by the status arrangements of his social group but rules will be tied to specific contexts and his autonomy will be limited.

I would like to add that it is entirely wrong to try to award points on this. It is absolute nonsense to say that if a boy has an elaborated code we give him seven out of ten, if he has a restricted code we give him five out of ten. A restricted code has an enormous potential; it has a potential of a different sort. Presumably what one would like to see is an individual having at his disposal a range of codes and a range of rôles which he is able to take up and explore imaginatively in terms of the social context in which he finds himself.

I think my fundamental interest, though we have not talked about it, is how the biological is transformed into the cultural, and one of the chief means is through language. This seems to me to be at the heart of socialization and to lie at the heart of the problem of how culture is transmitted.

David M. Downes

The Gang Myth

The notion of 'gang delinquency' is one of the most unkill-able and exotic in our culture. Whenever a small group of boys break and enter a warehouse, damage property or take and drive away private cars, the press reports usually speak of 'delinquent gangs' at work The term is used elastically to cover any group of more than two members. Any incident, from three youths yanking a cigarette machine off a wall to the mods' and rockers' riots, qualifies as 'gang delinquency'; it is also, in my view, thereby misreported and misunderstood.

Why bother so much about mere semantics? Who cares whether or not these acts of delinquency are committed by groups, cliques, mobs, gangs, crowds or whatever else they are called? Surely the delinquency is the main thing, and any other term is used simply to hive off the individual delin-quency from those who act collectively? But which word we choose to use from a host of alternatives usually tells us a great deal about the way people perceive an event or behaviour pattern, how they categorize it and, implicitly, their attitude towards it and what they think should be done about it. If (by any objective definition) the term 'gang' is used quite spuriously in connexion with delinquency, this involves a lot more than mere labelling for convenience's sake. It implies that a particular kind of delinquency is involved; that it takes a highly structured and recalcitrant form; that its participants are acting in a deliberately anti-social way not simply because they are doing wrong out of mischief or even malice, but because they believe that what they are doing is right. In short, the term 'gang' implies a set of delinquent values underlying the delinquent acts.

The word also differentiates delinquents from the rest of

us, not just as law-breakers or trouble-makers, but as almost a different species, cut off from the society with which they are implied to be at war, motivated by different needs and values, and controllable only by the severest of sanctions. Used in this way, and with these undertones, it is often simply a way of masking our lack of understanding of delinquency, or of adolescents, or more frequently of both together. But the word can be used sloppily by specialists as well as anybody else; take the following passage from one of the best pieces of research ever to be done on gang delinquency:

What is new apparently (say the authors, after asserting the age-old prevalence of the gang) is the

> extent to which gang delinquency has become a problem of major proportions in many countries since World War Two . . . United Nations and other reports suggest that collective forms of delinquency have become cause for alarm in such widely separated areas as Western Europe and the Iron Curtain countries, the Far East and Australia. . . . Picturesque names establish the public identity of these young people . . . names like 'zoot-suiters' and 'boppers' in the U.S., 'Teddy boys' in England . . . 'bodgies' (boys) and 'widgies' (girls) in Australia and New Zealand . . . the 'tap-karoschi' of Yugoslavia, and the 'lui-mang' and 'tai-pau' of Taiwan. Names the youngsters give themselves are even more intriguing – consider these *noms de plume* of lower class Negro gangs in Chicago: 'Jewtown Egyptian Cobras' the 'Vice Lords and Vice Ladies' and so on, down to the 'German Counts' with a swastika symbol.[1]

There are two main faults in this passage (which is really only a preamble to the very detailed analyses that follow in the book, but which gives a misleading impression of the nature of the delinquency problem at the outset). Firstly, gang delinquency and collective forms of delinquency are used as synonyms, when in fact gang delinquency is only one form of collective delinquency. And secondly, names conferred on forms of collective delinquency by the press, the adult community etc. (Teddy boys, 'bodgies' and 'widgies') are equated with names specific to American gangs proper (Jewtown Egyptian Cobras, etc.): though even in America it sometimes happens that names are adopted by gangs only when pressed for a label by police and social workers.[2] But the main point is that, even in a highly sophisticated study, the 'gang' problem is generalized with gay abandon to a world setting, and to the whole of history.

Research into gang delinquency in this country is in my view a fair reflection of its absence. To my knowledge, there have been only two attempts at systematic inquiry into the structure of delinquent groups – one in London by a clinical psychologist, the other in Exeter by an enterprising graduate student. My own work, which is on delinquency in two of the old East London boroughs, does touch on the subject; and a few articles and press reports have attempted something more critical than mere acceptance of the gang framework as an article of faith. Of course, absence of research into a subject is no guarantee of its insignificance. Gambling, for example, is a social phenomenon of great and growing importance, yet no research to speak of has been carried out on the subject, either in Europe or America. But for gangs a vast literature exists in the USA. It spans sixty years, from Herbert Asbury's bloodthirsty anecdotes of the gangs of New York and San Francisco[3] to the complex and highly theoretical work of James Short and his associates in Chicago today; and it takes in the classic of all gang literature, Frederick Thrasher's study of 1,313 delinquent gangs in Chicago in 1927.[4] To get similarly full-blooded pictures of gang life in England, one has to go back as far as Mayhew in the mid-nineteenth century,[5] or Arthur Morrison's 'Child of the Jago',[6] which describes the same period in what is now Shoreditch and Bethnal Green.

What research has been done in Britain implies a radically different group framework for delinquency from that portrayed in the American literature, though it is true that British work is limited to the mid-1950's and after. In the most systematic study so far, Dr Peter Scott, a psychiatrist at the Maudsley Hospital, interviewed 151 boys who were known to have committed group offences.[7] The results were published in 1956 – which was, after all, just about the heyday of the teddy-boy movement, which was supposed to have been, according to T. R. Fyvel's vivid study,[8] a gang phenomenon. Scott found that only 12 per cent of the boys could be described as members of 'gangs proper', and these were generally in the youngest age-group – between eight and thirteen. He defined the gang as a group with a leader, definite membership, persisting over time, and with definitely delinquent purposes; and he showed that far from supplying the bulk, or even the hard core, of his subjects, gangs barely figured at all as a significant factor on the delinquency scene. Yet the boys he interviewed were in a remand home, and generally this means that they were fairly serious offenders. The vast majority of them – 86 per cent – had offended in what Scott termed diffuse, or loosely structured, groups, whose usual activities were not delinquent, and which did not attempt to coerce any member into delinquent activity – a feature which is inconceivable in the 'gang proper'.

Scott's work provided the first real intimation that something was seriously amiss with the popular stereotype of 'gang warfare', which was trotted out by press and bench alike whenever some fracas or *mêlée* involving adolescents got more than usually out of hand. To some extent, this reaction was understandable during the heyday of the teddy-boy movement. In the last decade, we have become so inured to the excesses of teenage fashion that it is easy to forget the intensive bewilderment with which the adult world (and most adolescents) greeted the teddy-boy pioneers. The only precedent in living memory were the 'drape' suits of the early 1950's of which the teddy-boy gear was an extension. And of course, though we are now frequently reminded of Regency bucks, Georgian dandies, etc., most of the population in the mid-1950's had known little other than cloth caps and best dark suits all their lives. So as the style caught on, and more and more groups went 'Edwardian', they appeared to be a <u>sub-society</u>, openly and ostentatiously at variance with the social order. And, as they were caught up in the usual hooliganism and rowdyism and conflict with other teds or non-teds, the adult world took the new form for a new phenomenon, not simply of display, but of violence, vandalism and virility gone wrong. People reached for the nearest cliché and made it fit: gang warfare. As time went on, as the police and non-ted groups became anti-ted, it seems likely that the conflict situation actually did fuse some of the teds into gang-like postures, and the self-fulfilling prophecy worked its magic. Then the whole thing suddenly, inexplicably died, the gear began to look creased, shoddy and dated, and the teds went 'out'.

There was some excuse then: but what passes muster as a social reaction to the teds simply will not do as a reaction to the mods and rockers, ten years later and visibly more 'diffused' in groupings and mobility. Yet exactly the same responses – and sentences – were meted out. Magistrates surpassed themselves in eloquence – 'sawdust Caesars . . . hunting in packs', the voice of enraged Authority, indignant at being disturbed in the act of not thinking, the kind of voice which polarizes many adolescents into either timid conformity or recalcitrant toughness. The evidence, however, again points to the absence of 'gang warfare', woeful press exaggeration of the damage and injury done, and stereotyping so blatant that incidents quite unconnected with the original event were written up as mods–rockers 'clashes'.

Undoubtedly, a set of real events are there to be both explained and analysed: all that is being asserted here is that the 'gang' label once again obscured the events in question.[9]

Nevertheless, delinquent gangs were probably much commoner in this country up to and even after the Second World War than they are now. In his widely reported *New Society* article, 'Beat Killed the Gang',[10] Colin Fletcher argued, on the basis of personal experience, that gangs were prevalent in Liverpool until the mid-1950's. Then the growth of teenage culture and the great increase in adolescents' spending power diverted the energies and aspirations of 'the boys' into the legitimate fields of youth culture and away from the street-corner gang. Fletcher's analysis makes sense in more ways than one: the gang seems to be very much a phenomenon of the urban slum, which collects together the most deprived and exploited members of society at a great social distance from the more respectable areas and strata. The effect of teenage culture, and re-housing, was simultaneously to break down the parochial focus of slum adolescents' horizons, and to disperse them geographically. And both factors served to undermine the traditional gang framework. There is perhaps an even more fundamental reason why this should be so. The adolescent peer-group is, in most societies, a normal and necessary framework for youths. It occupies the stage between childhood dependence on parents, and the social responsibilities of adulthood. With their peers, that is, people of the same age, sex and status, adolescents really experience, for the first time, relationships embodying equality and democracy. The gang is a relatively authoritarian form of peer group, so that unless there are powerful reasons why they should take the gang form, adolescent peer groups are most likely to be fluid, demonstrative and egalitarian, rather than hierarchial and tightly knit. Hence, we often mistake 'peer-groups' for 'gang', and infer a 'structure' and 'hierarchy' which their members would themselves regard as ludicrous simply because of barriers to communicate between them and us when the group are both working class and occasionally delinquent.

Yet the gang myth survives, and it is resurrected at appropriate intervals. The mods' and rockers' riots, for instance, were reported as 'gang delinquency'. But an earlier example was the Finchley affray, the incident in which a boy was stabbed in a Finchley youth club after being sought out for some insult said to have been inflicted on a member of the 'Mussies', a couple of dozen boys from Muswell Hill in London. This case was heralded as 'gang warfare' by the bench and the press alike. The only exception was the *Observer* reporter, Christopher Brasher, who took the trouble to visit the cafés where the boys hung out, and critically examined the gang stereotype. He wrote:

> The fight was reported as a 'gang feud' between the 'Mussies' and the 'Finchley mob' ... The judge said: 'All of you have behaved in a way that would bring discredit on a pack of wolves ... This gang warfare has to be stamped out.' Yet in North London, as the police will tell you, the 'gangs' are no more than social gatherings in dance-halls and cafés of bored youths from the same area. They have no organization, no accepted leader, and no real name – they are just referred to as 'the mob from Highbury' or 'the mob from the Angel'. They seldom get out of hand, and their fights are usually restricted to a bash on the nose to settle an argument. But the danger is that anyone like Ron Fletcher (the leader of the 'Mussies', who was imprisoned for five years, and who was two or three years older than the rest) can quickly whip up a gang to 'turn over' any individual or group which has 'offended' him. Then the iron bars and the knives appear like magic.[11]

From Brasher's account, it is clear that the 'Mussies' constituted a 'gang' for the duration of the offence only; they were assembled virtually overnight by Fletcher from sheer acquaintances; and they would probably have dispersed anyway even if the police had not intervened so successfully. The crucial distinction to be drawn here is that between the 'gang' and what an American sociologist, Lewis Yablonsky, has called the 'near-group.'[12] The 'near-group' lacks persistence over time, and any consensus on membership; it is activated by a hard core of as few as two or three usually seriously disturbed boys who manipulate a large periphery of short-term members; and it acts through spontaneous mobilization for a single 'flare-up' rather than through protracted organization for gang conflict. Obviously, the Finchley affray, and the mods' and rockers' riots, are much closer to the 'near-group' conflict than the 'gang' warfare model.

This distinction may seem trifling to you if you are worried by delinquency but not by the niceties of how it happens. Given the fact of a messy conflict, who cares whether 'gangs' or 'near-groups' are involved? But the job of prevention and analysis make this kind of distinction of much more than purely academic interest. For example, Yablonsky has attacked the policy of New York street workers who treat 'near-groups' as gangs, and thereby generate a degree of real solidarity that never existed before 'prevention' got under way. To illustrate the disparity between the popular reports of gang war behaviour and their true organization, Yablonsky quotes from interviews with forty participants in what was reported in 1955 to be the biggest 'gang war' in New York's history. He found tremendous variation in the motives of the boys concerned and in their perceptions of the event itself. For example, estimates of the number involved ranged from eighty to 5,000; reasons given for fighting varied from 'Didn't have anything to do' to 'They always picked on us'; and so on. Yablonsky reconstructs the event as '. . . not a social situation of two structured teenaged armies meeting on a battlefield to act out a defined situation; it was a case of two near-groups in action.' The situation in the United States is still being unravelled; but it looks as if there is a great diversity of group frameworks for serious delinquency, from

structured gangs to near-groups. In this country we appear
to have a much narrower range of variation; gangs are virtually non-existent, but mobilization of 'near-groups' is possible in extreme situations. In the Exeter study I have already
referred to, M. R. Farrant located just this pattern, of '... five
groups (of a few members each) which were in fact leadership
nuclei of larger "quasi-groups"'; and these quasi-groups were
mobilized and fused into a gang-like solidarity only on very
rare occasions of extreme stress.'[13]

Now, if we accept Fletcher's view that the disappearance
of the gang framework has left the seriously disturbed delinquent isolated, it follows that sporadic outbreaks of 'near-group'
conflict will be high-lighted much more than in the past – for
the seriously disturbed individual was then assimilated into
the relative normality of the traditional gang. This means that
if we want to prevent delinquency we should concentrate on
locating these seriously disturbed adolescents and attempt to
get them referred for social psychiatric treatment, rather than
adopt social group work techniques and try to re-socialize the
'near-group' as a unity through its so-called 'leader'. Obviously, this type of leader has emerged in a situation of conflict. If we divert the group's energies as a group into more
conventional fields we undermine his leadership, and render
his position even more desperate. This can lead to his project-
ing the group into an extreme delinquent situation in order
to reaffirm his status.[14] To my mind, the most valuable
function of the so-called 'detached workers' is not so much
to organize delinquent groups and channel their energies,
as to find out what is going on, and document the reality –
to act, in fact, as a communication link.[15]

But once we have disentangled the occasional 'near-group'
outbreak from the delinquency pattern as a whole, we are left
with the rather unspectacular reality of thousands of small
cliques who are from time to time engaged in often quite
serious forms of delinquency; but this is essentially a phase

they will out-grow, and they do not appear to contain any more psychiatric abnormality than you would find in the normal population. These tend to be what Brasher called 'social gatherings ... of bored youths'. But how does the gang myth help to distort our understanding of these adolescents, and why is it perpetuated in the face of all the evidence to the contrary?

First, the gang myth makes their occasional delinquencies appear much more purposeful and systematic than they actually are, so that when we try to understand them we stress their differences from the more conventional members of society, almost to the point of abnormality, and we tend to overlook their similarities, in values, tastes and aspirations. This means that we cannot accept that they drift into delinquency; rather we see them as being marauders, committed to law-breaking as a 'way of life'. Secondly, this conveniently deflects us from our real task, which is to tackle the roots of their fatalism; these lie in the poor job opportunities, the run-down slum schools, the social hypocrisy, they sense when the rhetoric of equality in our society clashes blatantly with their sole experience of inequality. On one point I would like to develop Fletcher's thesis a little further. If 'beat' has killed the gang (or at least delivered the final blow of a slow, long-term dissolution) it certainly has not killed delinquency. Perhaps this is because those adolescents who are most conspicuously successful in the world of teenage culture are not builder's labourers and van-boys, but those who would have been socially mobile and relatively successful anyway, ex-art-students, for example. If one adopts David Matza's idea[16] that there are essentially three types of adolescent protest – delinquency, bohemianism and radicalism – then the effect of teenage culture seems to have been an increase in bohemianism at the expense of radicalism, but not at the expense of delinquency. But it is misleading to suggest that the values of teenage culture are intrinsically delinquent – or even 'delinquescent' – that is, potentially delinquent. They are no more delinquent in themselves than the values of an Oxford high table or a board-room meeting. But teenage culture does generate goals and aspirations, and the divergence between these unreal goals and the drabness of real life could periodically erupt into a search for 'kicks', and lead to supposedly 'motiveless' delinquency. Bohemianism is just as likely a response, especially among middle-class adolescents. The two are far too often confused in adult minds – 'beatniks' and 'mods and rockers' are not equally anti-social. But both are protest rôles only intermittently played out by their incumbents, who most of the time act quite conventionally.

In conclusion, teenage culture provides yet another area of discontinuity in the experience of the lower-working-class boy; and it may have increased delinquency by creating a new hierarchy of success in leisure in which he is, as in work and education, at the 'bottom of the heap'. But we would not expect the gang to re-emerge as a result of these pressures. This would probably only happen if new slums are created for, in particular, the immigrant communities; or if mass unemployment returns to the adolescent job market. Instead, we would expect an intensification of delinquency, but in intermittent and mundane forms, with the occasional 'near-group' outbreak. By perpetuating the gang myth, we fail to see the direction in which delinquency is moving, and as a result we fail to see the lessons it can teach us about the quality and faults of our society as a whole.

REFERENCES

1 Short, J. F. and Strodtbeck, F. L. *Group process and gang delinquency* (University of Chicago Press, 1965, pp. 1–2).
2 Yablonsky, L. *The violent gang* (Collier-Macmillan, 1962; Penguin Books, 1967).
3 Asbury, H. *The gangs of New York: an informal history of the underworld* (Knopf, 1928). Asbury evokes a world of turbulent

gang warfare and urban corruption in a style which invites comparison with Mayhew, though he lacks Mayhew's range of interest and power of detailed social description. Asbury optimistically assumed that in 1928 'his day (the adult gangster's) has simply passed' (Introduction, p. xiv), though he stresses later on that 'there are as many juvenile gangs in New York today as there have ever been ... but in general they have become much less criminal' (p. 246).

4 Thrasher, F. M. *The gang: a study of gangs in Chicago* (University of Chicago Press, 1927; abridged with new introduction by J. F. Short, 1963).

5 Mayhew, H. *London's underworld*; ed. by P. Quennell (Spring Books, 1958).

6 Morrison, A. *A child of the Jago* (Methuen, 1896).

7 Scott, P. D. 'Gangs and delinquent groups in London' in *British Journal of Delinquency*, Vol. 7. July 1956, pp. 8–21.

8 Fyvel, T. R. *The insecure offender: rebellious youth in the welfare state* (Chatto & Windus, 1961).

9 Cohen, S. 'Mods, rockers and the rest; community reactions to juvenile delinquency' in *The Howard Journal*, 1967, pp. 121–30. The most perceptive account and analysis so far of the 'mods–rocker riots'.

10 New Society. *Youth in 'New Society'*; ed. by T. Raison (Hart-Davis, 1966).

11 Brasher, C. 'Turning 'em over in Finchley' in the *Observer*, 15 July, 1962.

12 Yablonsky, L. 'The delinquent gang as a near-group' in *Social Problems*, Vol. 7, No. 2. Fall, 1959; and in *The violent gang* (op. cit.).

13 Farrant, M. R. in the *Guardian*, 14 September 1965.

14 Short, J. F. and Strodtbeck, F. L., op. cit., Chap. 8. *The response of gang leaders to status threats.*

15 Goetschius, G. W. and Tash, M. J. *Working with unattached youth* (Routledge, 1967). An extensively documented and much more ambitious account of 'detached' work with adolescents.

16 Matza, D. 'Subterranean traditions of American youth' in The American Academy of Political and Social Science *Teenage Culture*; ed. by J. Bernard (Annals of the Academy, Vol. 338, 1961, pp. 102–18); see also his *Delinquency and drift* (Wiley, 1964).